GULF COAST COMMUNITY COLLEGE
LIBRARY
5230 West Hwy. 98
Panama City, Florida 32401

Career Game Plan for Student-Athletes

Jennifer Bohac

Prentice Hall
Upper Saddle River, New Jersey 07458

Library of Congress Cataloging-in-Publication Data
Bohac, Jennifer, 1964–
   Career game plan for student athletes / Jennifer Bohac.
     p. cm.
   Includes bibliographical references (p. 190) and index.
   ISBN 0-13-082278-7
   1. Vocational guidance—United States. 2. College athletes—
–Employment—United States. I. Title.
  HF5382.5.UB64 2000
  331.7'0235'0973—dc21   99-14675
                                                                   CIP

Publisher: *Carol Carter*
Managing Editor: *Mary Carnis*
Acquisitions Editor: *Sue Bierman/Sande Johnson*
Manufacturing Buyer: *Marc Bove*
Director of Manufacturing & Production: *Bruce Johnson*
Production Editor: *Adele Kupchik*
Editorial Assistant: *Michelle M. Williams*
Marketing Manager: *Jeff McIlroy*
Formatting/Page Make-up: *Julie Boddorf*
Cover designer: *Bruce Kenselaar*
Art Director: *Jayne Conte*
Associate Art Director: *Marianne Frasco*
Senior Design Coordinator: *Miguel Ortiz*
Image Permissions Supervisor: *Kay Dellosa*
Photo Researcher: *Michelle M. Williams*
Permissions Assistant: *Anthony Arabia*
Printer/Binder: *Victor Graphics*
Copy Editor: *Lynn Buckingham*

©2000 by Prentice-Hall, Inc.
Upper Saddle River, New Jersey 07458

*All rights reserved. No part of this book may be
reproduced, in any form or by any means,
without permission in writing from the publisher.*

Printed in the United States of America

10 9 8 7 6 5 4 3 2 1

ISBN 0-13-082278-7

Prentice-Hall International (UK) Limited, *London*
Prentice-Hall of Australia Pty. Limited, *Sydney*
Prentice-Hall Canada Inc., *Toronto*
Prentice-Hall Hispanoamericana, S.A., *Mexico*
Prentice-Hall of India Private Limited, *New Delhi*
Prentice-Hall of Japan, Inc., *Tokyo*
Pearson Education Asia Pte. Ltd., *Singapore*
Editora Prentice-Hall do Brasil, Ltda., *Rio de Janeiro*

To those who support me, believe in me, and love me, I dedicate this work. It represents the culmination of a long journey.

To my mom and dad, Florine and Willie Bohac: your lifelong love, support, encouragement, and sacrifice have been an inspiration. I have reached the pinnacle of a dream and I dedicate it to you.

Contents

Preface ix
Acknowledgments xi
About the Author xiii

1 Transitioning Out of Sports and Remaining Competitive — 1

Introduction 1
Student-Athlete "Life after Sport" 2
Professional Athletes 5
Student-Athlete to Employee 6
Student-Athlete's Guide to Understanding and Identifying Transferable Skills 11
Conclusion 12
Activity 12

2 Conducting Your Personal Assessment and Exploring Career Options — 14

Introduction 14
Self-Assessment 15
Career Assessment 25
Informational Interviewing and Career Shadowing 29
Conclusion and Activity 34

3 Assessing Your Marketability and Planning a Job Search Strategy — 35

Introduction 35
Résumé Worksheet 36

Four-year Career Planning 36
Career Planning Advice 42
Job Search Strategies 43
Job Search Marketing Plan 45
Organizing and Conducting a Job Search 46
Employers Look for Specific Traits 51
Preparing for an Interview 52
Employer's Expectations 54
Reaching Your Goal 55
Using the Telephone to Find and Get the Job You Want 55
Conclusion and Activity 59

4 Writing a Résumé and Organizing a Portfolio 60

Introduction 60
Résumé Writing: Making a Good First Impression 61
The College Student's Résumé 62
Résumé Preparation 64
The Scannable Résumé 71
Action Words That Create Strong Impact 74
Final Résumé Pointers 77
The Portfolio 78
Conclusion 80
Activity 80

5 Networking 82

Introduction 82
Networking the Right Way 83
Making New Contacts 83
Meeting with Contacts 84
Network Maintenance Tips 85
Effective Networking Skills 86
Surviving a Networking Event 88
Networking Exercise 89
Requesting Letters of Recommendation 89
Conclusion 91
Activity 91

6 Researching Employers — 93

Introduction   93
How to Research Companies and Employers   94
Researching the Job Market, Career Fields, and Industries   97
Using Research Information for Successful Interviews   99
Conclusion   101

7 Writing the Cover Letter — 102

Introduction   102
Using Cover Letters   103
Tips for Effective Cover Letters   105
The Reality of Cover Letters   109
Job Applications   109
Activity   111

8 Presenting Yourself: Dress and Decorum — 112

Introduction   112
Dress for Success   113
Business Etiquette   114
Conclusion   117
Activity   117

9 Interviewing and Following Up — 118

Introduction   118
The Seven Phases of an Interview   119
Preinterview Personal Reflection Questions   120
First Impressions   122
Establishing the Relationship   124
The Interview   124
Frequently Asked Questions   127
Scoring Points on Tough Questions   129
Responding to Negative Questions   134
Questions to Ask the Interviewer   137
Prove It!   138
The Art of Storytelling   139
Final Checklist   142

Decorum 143
Tips from On-Campus Recruiters 144
Types of Interviews 145
Are You Ready for a Behavioral Interview? 147
Behavioral Questions Worksheet 149
The Second Visit or What Is a Site Visit? 152
Interview Follow-up: What It Is and Why It's Needed 155
Dealing with Rejection in the Job Search 158
Conclusion 159
Activity 159

10 Using Technology in Your Job Search — 160

Introduction 160
The Internet 161
Career Web Sites 163
Conclusion 170
Activity 170

11 Gaining Professional Experience — 171

Introduction 171
Professional Experience Programs 172
Internships and Co-ops 173
Conclusion 175

12 Negotiating Salary and Benefits — 176

Introduction 176
Where to Find Salary Information 177
Negotiating Your Compensation 178
Weighing Compensation 179
Multiple Job Offers 180
Responding to a Job Offer 182
Relocation: Should You Make the Move? 187
Conclusion 188
Activity 189

References — 190

Index — 191

Preface

As a student-athlete, you have committed a great deal of time, energy, sweat, and tears toward gaining success in your sport. The high level of commitment that you dedicated to athletics has obviously paid off for you. Your dedication allowed you to participate at the collegiate level and you proudly represent your college or university. Your success is proof that hard work ultimately culminates in positive results.

Some of you will continue with your sport upon graduation from college. A startling statistic, however, is the fact that approximately only three percent of college student-athletes continue into professional sports. That may be a frightening thought if you consider yourself a member of the 97 percent that will not enter the realm of professional athletics.

The transition from being in your sport to the period when your athletic involvement is not an intricate part of your life may be a difficult one. Think of the many hours that you spend practicing, training, participating in team meetings, competing and traveling to rival schools. Try to calculate the amount of time that you dedicate each week to your pursuit of victory in your sport. For most of you, this more than likely is a forty-hour per week "job."

The world of work is a huge unknown for you at this time, but just as you have committed your time and energy to your sport, it is now time to commit those same resources to your job search. You are well prepared for this activity, especially considering you already understand the dedication required of a forty-hour work week. Now, you need to transfer the skills you learned as a student-athlete in the world of sport to the world of work. The skills you have already mastered plus some new skills you'll learn from this book will make you prepared for this challenge.

This book highlights the skills you have already gained (chapter 1) and presents some new skills that are specific to career planning and development. What if you have not decided what career path you would like to follow? Chapter 2 addresses this issue and provides many resources that can assist you in clarifying your career goals.

After deciding upon potential careers, the next task is to establish a job search marketing plan (chapter 3). The job search marketing plan is your road map that will help you track your goals as you move toward finding a satisfying career. Networking (chapter 5) is one of the most successful ways to find available positions that match your marketing plan. You already have an established network, especially through your sport, and this chapter will discuss how to expand your network and utilize it for your job search.

Writing a résumé (chapter 4) and cover letter (chapter 7) are required skills for a successful job search. In order to get your foot in the door for an interview, your résumé and cover letter must be in perfect condition. Before you enter an interview, you will need to research the employer (chapter 6). This research has a dual purpose. First, it allows you to find out more about the company and industry so you can decide if this is an appropriate work environment for you. Secondly, it will provide you the information you need to answer and ask questions during the interview. Appropriate attire and etiquette for the interview are the focus of chapter 8, while chapter 9 discusses the interview process itself.

Technology is growing at a faster rate than ever anticipated. The Internet is an excellent resource when conducting a job search and is discussed in chapter 10. Many employers are seeking candidates who have high-quality computer skills. Working with the Internet can assist you in this manner. Likewise, employers are also looking for candidates who possess career-related work skills. These skills can be gained through internships, cooperative education, and summer employment (chapter 11). Finally, deciding how much you are worth and the skills you need to conduct an effective salary negotiation are discussed in chapter 12.

The skills that you gain from this book will be used not only as you graduate from college but also as you conduct future job searches during your lifetime. Therefore, consider the topics discussed in this book as lifetime career development skills.

This book requires your participation. There are many worksheets and activities found throughout the text. In order to get the most out of the topics discussed in this book, you must dedicate the time and commitment required to complete these activities. A job search is an important aspect of your life and it requires the same amount of dedication as your sport. As in sports, this level of dedication will ultimately result in success.

Acknowledgments

I would like to express my appreciation to the following people for their support, encouragement, and guidance:

To my staff in the Career Services for Student-Athletes and my colleagues in the Career Center and Athletic Department for being so supportive throughout this endeavor.

A special thank-you to Karen Rupp and Rebecca Moody of Texas A&M for their contributions.

To Stephanie Fenley for her assistance and support.

To the staff at Prentice Hall, I am grateful for your belief and support, especially Sue Bierman, Michelle Williams, Kevin Witt, and the rest of the Prentice Hall family.

To my other friends and colleagues too numerous to mention, both at Texas A&M and throughout the country, for their support and encouragement.

To the Texas A&M student-athletes who have been in my classes and have impacted the development of this material.

Thank you all.

Reviewers

Vincent Martin	University of Tennessee, Knoxville
Kate Riffee	Ohio State University
Pam Overton	Florida State University
Keith Zimmer	University of Nebraska, Lincoln
Patsy Livingston	Point Loma Nazarene University

About the Author
—JENNIFER BOHAC

Jennifer Bohac is Assistant Director for Athletic Services at the Texas A&M Career Center. The major focus of the program is to assist student-athletes in finding temporary jobs during vacation periods, internship positions related to their major, and professional employment upon graduation. In addition, the program provides one-on-one career counseling with student-athletes as well as providing workshops, mock-interviews, and résumé and career planning assistance. Jennifer also has the responsibility of monitoring the summer job program, NCAA employment compliance, job development, teaching the course "Career Development for Student-Athletes," and more.

Jennifer is the faculty advisor for Squadron One of the Corps of Cadets. She was named the Outstanding Faculty Advisor for the Corps for the 1994–1995 academic year. She is active on campus serving as an advisor for the Ladies Leadership Organization, Mentor for the Leadership in Medicine Program and past president of the University Advisors and Counselors.

Some of Jennifer's community activities include past-president of the Brazos County A&M Club, Chamber of Commerce Activities and Committees, College Station Noon Lions Club—president, Aggie Hostel, & Bryan City Council Committees.

Jennifer recently received a Ph.D. in Higher Education Administration in May 1998 from Texas A&M University. She also obtained a Masters in Education Administration, as well as bachelors' degrees in Animal Science and Agricultural Economics at A&M. Her research is on occupational progress and career planning of former football players of the Big 12 Conference.

Chapter 1
Transitioning Out of Sports and Remaining Competitive

INTRODUCTION

As a student-athlete, there are probably lots of ways that your athletic involvement gets in the way of your career planning process. The National Collegiate Athletic Association (NCAA) limits the amount of employment you can obtain during the school year, and practices and training take most, if not all, of your free time. On the other hand, your athletic involvement gives you many advantages that students who are not athletes do not get the opportunity to experience.

What, you may be thinking, could those advantages possibly be? You have had the opportunity to prove your leadership skills, whether it was on the field, in the pool, or on the court. You have had the opportunity to work as a member of a team, and you understand the dynamics of success when every team member contributes to the good of the whole. You have had the opportunity to expand your network across state and sometimes national borders. Think of all the coaches, players, trainers, and fans you have met since you started your career as an athlete. These individuals now make up your career network and you can utilize them as references and resources during your job search.

As you can see, there are many advantages to being a student-athlete. This chapter explains more of those in depth and also discusses the transition that most of you will encounter when your athletic career comes to a close.

Student-Athlete "Life after Sport"

Easing the Transition

Ultimately, all student-athletes will reach the point where their competitive collegiate careers will draw to an end. Some will be ready for this transition and others will not. No matter how the student-athlete feels, there may be many changes to cope with—especially loss.

Student-athletes may experience a series of emotional, physical, social, and mental changes that will differ in intensity and impact, depending on the individual. Coping mechanisms may include denial, isolation, substance abuse, or other negative behaviors. Retirement from sports is not easy—even if a student-athlete is ready. A transition that is prepared for and welcomed, however, will usually generate less stress than one that is viewed negatively.

The NCAA has developed techniques that help prepare athletes for this transition. The activities that follow are recommended by the NCAA for groups of student-athletes exploring career development together, along with an experienced facilitator.

Activities

1. Defining "Transition" (Optional)

    ✓ Create a common definition of the word *transition*

    This activity is designed to help create a common framework from which to work. It allows the group to recognize commonalities and consistencies among the participants regarding this topic. It also helps the facilitators begin to identify the individual needs and concerns of each athlete.

Brainstorm activity:

What does the word *transition* mean to you? (List examples: change, exciting, scary, etc.) Discuss these.

2. Experimental Activity

    ✓ Group activity (icebreaker): Gordon Knot

    This activity serves to further break down the barriers between individual student-athletes and the various teams represented at any one seminar. It is designed to be a fun movement-oriented activity that serves to simulate team interaction and allows for individual reflection around team concept, individual and team orientation, and competition versus cooperation in the workplace (as compared to the athletic arena).

    Activity: Have groups of four to eight people get into a circle and grasp hands across the group. The task is to totally untangle the group while not letting go of each other's hands. Allow ten to twelve minutes. Discuss individual and group behavior and feelings after the activity.

3. Discussion with Former College and/or Professional Athlete(s): "Withdrawal from Competition and Adjustment to Worklife"

    This activity brings the real-life experiences of a former athlete to the group. Issues, expectations, and realities of adjustment to life after sport are discussed in a frank and open manner. Discussion with a former student-athlete reinforces the importance of early exploration of appropriate preventative coping mechanisms.

4. Understanding and Identifying Transferable Skills

    Each student-athlete has an individual set of skills that have been developed and enhanced through participation in sport. Many student-athletes do not recognize that many of these skills can be of real benefit in the workplace and beyond. Individual reflection and an examination of the demands of the sport experience help to identify the functional skills of each student-athlete.

    Activity:

    a) Have the student-athletes independently complete the "Transferable Skills" (page 13)

    b) Have them form diads and compare answers

    c) Report to group on similarities and differences

d) Emphasize qualities and characteristics learned from athletics and how to let employers know you have these skills—you have to sometimes educate employers on the subject.

Discussion:

Have you developed these skills?
How important to your success were they?
How would potential employers know you have these skills?
How can you emphasize your skills?
How can you develop the skills that are missing?

5. Exploring Work Values

This activity utilizes an interactive activity, which requires each individual to examine his or her life values and their importance in identifying a fulfilling work experience. Each student-athlete will complete the questions designed to stimulate exploration of career needs and goals.

Activity:

a) Ask students to prioritize the five most important work values
b) Are there patterns that exist?
c) Do your very important work values fit your goals for career?
d) Which are negotiable? Which do you need now? Later?

6. Success on Your First Job

Once you have gotten a job, several issues arise that may need to be addressed, including appropriate mechanisms for identification and attainment of fulfilling and autonomous work.

a) Advancement opportunities
b) Responsibility and recognition
c) Autonomy in work
d) Flexibility
e) Use of special abilities and background
f) Rewards (different from those of sport)
g) Loyalty and commitment to employer
h) Others . . .

7. Developing New and Fulfilling Interests

Student-athletes are encouraged to begin to explore new hobbies, lifetime sports, and other interests beyond their current sport. Resources (work, community, recreational, and voluntary) are identified, and the importance of developing and/or reinforcing support systems is discussed.

SOURCE: *NCAA Life Skills Career Development Notebook: Life After Sports*

Professional Athletes

What These Workers Do

Highly athletic people might want to consider getting a job as a "pro" athlete. They should know, however, that very few athletes ever make it that far. It's a good idea, then, to have another job in mind as well. Professional athletes include baseball, basketball, football, and tennis players, golfers, ice skaters, skiers, stock car drivers, rodeo riders, and anyone playing a sport for money.

Professional athletes play sports in front of an audience and get paid for it. Fans enjoy seeing these athletes play so much that they are willing to pay to watch a game or match. Professional athletes are performers or entertainers, a lot like musicians and actors. They must perform well in each game or risk losing each game. If they don't play well, they won't last long in this job.

What the Job Is Like

The work of professional athletes is very demanding, both physically and mentally; therefore, they must be in the best possible shape. Most modern athletes work out all year, both during the season and in the off-season. They must be able to perform their jobs at the highest level at all times. Professional athletes also face the constant threat of injuries—especially in contact sports—that could end their careers. For these and other reasons, this kind of job can be quite stressful.

During the regular season, professional athletes often practice two or three hours a day. They may have other duties related to the team as well, such as attending meetings or watching films about the opposition. Athletes often move to the places where their team is located. If management decides to trade them, they may have to move again. At least in team sports, professional athletes often have curfews and other restrictions on what they can and can't do in their personal lives. They can't just "leave the job at the office" like workers in other professions can.

Student-Athlete to Employee

Ten Qualities of Team Players

These personal strengths, acquired through sports participation, are desirable in virtually all jobs, regardless of the field:

1. ***Ability to organize time well.*** Student-athletes must balance a full-time academic workload, a full-time commitment to athletics, and other campus activities. Appreciate the time management skills you have developed.

2. ***Ability to work well with others.*** Through athletic team membership, most student-athletes become very familiar with the experience of working toward group goals. Athletics teaches that it is sometimes necessary to submerge one's ego and personal goals into the goals of the organization - and that leadership is the ability to get people to work as a team.

3. ***Goal directedness.*** Student-athletes develop the ability to concentrate their energies and attention over an extended period of time and to block out distractions while they proceed toward their goals.

4. ***Competitiveness.*** The competitive spirit is the lifeblood of the athletic experience. Student-athletes gain experience in the rigors of winning and losing, and they look forward to the opportunity to fight more battles, test their abilities, and risk their self-esteem against tough opposition. This is a strong asset in most jobs.

5. ***Confidence.*** Student-athletes are continually in situations where they must pump up and believe in their own power to produce effectively under pressure. The ability to approach tough performance situations with the belief that you'll do well is crucial. Practice in maintaining self-confidence, especially under tense circumstances, can carry over to on-the-job challenges.

6. ***Persistence and endurance.*** Athletics is often characterized by long and hard work toward distant rewards and by the ability to wring a maximum effort from yourself whenever necessary. This

may include playing while in pain or, in general, performing under adverse circumstances. Athletics teaches intensity of effort and the belief that sufficient preparation and determination will eventually pay off.

7. ***Loyalty.*** Loyalty emerges from the bond an individual student-athlete builds with his or her team and is expressed in the willingness to support team efforts under any circumstances. Loyalty contributes to the morale of a team or work group, because it enables each team member to trust that others will work toward the same ends.

8. ***Discipline.*** Organizing one's time, adhering to guidelines, giving maximum effort on a regular basis, concentrating one's energies, and screening out competing priorities are all necessary in athletics. The systematic application of one's energies toward a desired goal is highly valued in any work setting.

9. ***Ability to take criticism.*** Because their performance on the field is watched closely, student-athletes are accustomed to taking criticism. Coaches recommend changes and force athletes to cope with the feeling that they could have done better. Student-athletes typically develop into good listeners when constructive criticism is offered because they recognize its value in helping them advance toward overall goals.

10. ***Resilience.*** Sports offers continued opportunities to test oneself, succeed or fail, and then come back for more. No one who competes in a sport can avoid the experience of failure. Student-athletes learn to face yesterday's failure and bury any negative feelings because tomorrow's contest demands their full attention. Among the most valuable lessons of athletics are how to win, how to lose, and how to rebound from both.

Advice from Those Who Know

You aren't alone in your job search. Many student-athletes have encountered the same concerns and questions that you are probably having now. Wouldn't it be nice to look into a crystal ball and see what the future will hold? Unfortunately that can't be done, but the second-best alternative is to follow advice given by those people who have been there before. A study was recently conducted of former student-athletes who played football in the Big 12 Conference. The suggestions they make and the advice they give is invaluable. Following are some of their words of wisdom:

On Choosing a Major and/or Career:

- Choose something that will allow you to do the things you enjoy.
- Try to get into something you enjoy and don't worry about how much money you think that degree will bring you.
- Find out exactly what you like and do it! Don't do something because it seems popular or it might be easier.
- Be patient in choosing a career. Remember a very select few play pro sports, so it is very important to make the correct choice.
- Find a career that interests you as soon as you begin college and plan your degree and electives in a way so you can succeed at the career once you graduate. Don't wait until your third or fourth year to plan a lifetime career.

On Extracurricular Activities:

- Plan for the future. Be as involved as possible with activities outside of sports.
- Once you declare your major and/or focus on one subject area, look for extracurricular activities (non-athletic related) that can enhance your understanding of the career you desire.
- Meet as many alumni as possible. Get involved in clubs on campus that interest you.
- I wished earlier in my college career that I had been involved with other groups in the college atmosphere besides athletics. I learned a lot from other students and organizations, and they get a chance to meet an athlete up close and personal. It's a chance to develop a good reputation, if you earn it.

On Getting Experience:

- Explore all opportunities. Get as much work experience as possible.
- Get a summer job and/or internship before graduation. It may help you out tremendously in getting you started after graduation.
- Try to find an internship in your chosen field of study to ensure that it is the field you want to be in.
- Get applicable summer jobs and keep track of every businessperson you know.

- Education, internships, work experience, and personal contacts are very important in facilitating a career of your choice. Focus and direction within those opportunities are equally important.

On Networking:

- Network early and often.
- Make as many degree-related contacts as you can; in the end, as long as you get good grades, it's not what you know but whom you know that counts.
- Work closely with the departments in your field to establish contacts and references.
- Meet as many people as possible while you're in the "limelight." These contacts may pay off later.
- Be nice to alumni, speak to them, get to know them. Typically, the alumni who are active in the program are successful people. These people can really help you, and there is no better opportunity to have an audience with them than when you're actually playing.
- Spend time with professionals to see what their jobs are like. Even if there is no money in it for you, learning from real life is better than from any book.
- Talk to people in your field of interest. Most people are willing to talk to you and offer advice. This also helps you to decide if a field or job is right for you.

On Using Campus Resources:

- Don't be afraid to seek help if there are things you can't do or don't understand. Use your advisors and university personnel.
- Find out all you can about your career. Take full advantage of any assistance that your institution offers in career planning.
- Seek mentors; take your education as seriously as you take your athletic careers. Education is an investment in your future.
- Be sure to get extensive counseling on the types of employment that will best suit your particular area of study.
- Spend enough time in career assessment and talking to an advisor early on to have a clear picture of the appropriate coursework to pursue. Get to know all of your professors and have the mindset that there will not be a pro career after graduating.

- Don't waste time; prepare, decide early on your route, and meet with the appropriate advisor.

On Combining Athletics and Academics

- Do not count on people to spoon-feed you when you get out of school. Go to class and study. Make the most of your education while you're in school.
- Be a *student*-athlete, not just an athlete. When your job performance is being evaluated, nobody will care how many tackles you made.
- Strike a balance between academic responsibilities and athletics. Assume that you won't play professional sports and plan accordingly.
- Think long term. Enjoy college but remember you are setting the foundation for the rest of your life!
- Use the wonderful opportunity college offers to your full advantage. Always remember, your physical ability will one day falter but your mind can carry you much farther. You are in school for one reason and that is to get an education. Graduation should always be your first priority in college.
- Study, study, study; take your schoolwork seriously and make connections within your field.

These former student-athletes were also asked, "How did your undergraduate education help your career?" Here are some of their responses:

- It developed communication, analytical, leadership/management skills.
- It reinforced the value of hard work.
- It gave me an appreciation and general understanding of a broad range of topics. It gave me the ability to converse with a broad range of people.
- It has helped me obtain consistent career advancements on a yearly interval.
- It helped me to get my first job and helped me to develop the work ethic and problem-solving skills necessary to do my job.
- It taught me excellent project management and problem solving skills.
- A college degree will open many doors to opportunity throughout the rest of my life—the degree shows that I set a goal and achieved it.

- It taught me how to reason and how to work with others. At times, I think the development of my social skills was a greater benefit than the actual formal education.

Student-Athlete's Guide to Understanding and Identifying Transferable Skills

This worksheet is designed to help you identify personal characteristics and skills you have developed through sports participation, which may be transferable to the workplace. List at least five answers to each of the following questions:

1. What personal qualities and characteristics do you think are important for athletic achievement?

2. What personal qualities and strengths have helped you succeed in sports?

3. What have you learned from competitive situations?

▲ Conclusion

The transition from the world of sports to the world of work will be a challenging one. You are already equipped with many of the skills and talents that you need, however, to make this transition a success.

The remainder of this book will assist you in some skill areas that you may not have already mastered, such as writing a résumé, researching potential employers, interviewing for a job, and negotiating salary. As a student-athlete, you already know how to win. The skills you gain from this book will show you how to actively search for and obtain a winning career.

▲ Activity

Make a list of all the skills you have gained as a result of participation in your sport. Don't leave anything out, because you never know what skills might come in handy during your job search. Once you have these skills listed, think of two ways that each of these skills will assist you either at the job or while conducting a job search. You will be pleasantly surprised at the number of skills you already possess.

Activity 13

Transferable Skills

	Important for Succeeding in Sports	Important for Succeeding in the Workplace	Skills I Have	Skills I Need to Develop	Comments
Making a commitment and sticking with it					
Learning to win and lose					
Working with people you don't necessarily like					
Learning patience					
Becoming disciplined					
Being fit					
Learning respect					
Learning to be creative					
Learning to take orders					
Learning self-control					
Learning communication skills					
Learning drive and dedication—pushing yourself to the limit					
Learning your limitations					
Learning to compete without hatred					
Accepting complete responsibility for your behavior					
Learning to commit a great deal of time and effort					
Ability to accept criticism and feedback in order to learn					
Learning to take risks					
Developing a sense of accomplishment					
Learning to be flexible					
Learning to perform under pressure					
Positioning yourself for success					

Chapter 2
Conducting Your Personal Assessment and Exploring Career Options

INTRODUCTION

"What are you going to do when you graduate?" This is a question you have probably heard many times before. For some people, it is an easy question to answer. These people have known, ever since they were small children, what they wanted to do for a living. For other people, this question is not as simple. Some people can think of lots of things they want to do, and they find it nearly impossible to narrow their choice down to one field. For still others, this question is difficult because they cannot think of anything that they are interested in enough to spend the rest of their life doing it.

One of the first steps in answering this question is learning a little bit more about yourself. What is important to you? What things do you like to do? What are you good at? Do you like to work alone or as a member of a team? Do you work best with people, ideas, or things? These are all questions that you should consider before you start to consider different fields of work.

Your values, your interests, your personality and your skills will play a major role in determining your career and your future. Without evaluating these, it will be very difficult for you to make a decision about a college major or a job. This chapter provides many resources to assist you in your self-assessment. And, with advances in technology, many resources can be found on the Internet or in computer software packages which this chapter will also address. Making a career decision is a long path to follow, but learning about yourself along the road will make the traveling that much easier.

Self-Assessment

To a large degree, maximum success in choosing a satisfying and lasting career depends on how well you make a self-inventory by evaluating your skills, abilities, and interests. Conducting an effective self-inventory is not an easy task. You have to examine your entire life's activities. It requires an individual reflective effort, as well as guidance from family, counselors, and teachers. It may include taking appropriate tests. The following information is provided to assist you in your self-assessment.

Take a moment and think about the following questions: *What do you like doing? How do you spend your time? What are your natural talents and abilities? What do you do best? What do you like doing the most? What skills do you already have from previous experiences that may qualify you for new jobs? What are your unique traits and characteristics? What is important to you? What do you need in your career to stay motivated and energized? Do you really know yourself?*

Self-assessment is important, both in choosing a major and in conducting a job search. You will want to choose a major that fits your interests and that will help you achieve your career goals. Later, you must be able to describe yourself and express your goals clearly and concisely to prospective employers.

How do you begin setting goals? First of all, remember that goals must be **SMART:**

Specific
Measurable
Attainable
Results Oriented
Time Bound

Therefore, you might begin by completing the statement, "I will [state what you plan to do] by [specify a date]." Then list the steps you will take to accomplish your goal, what you hope the results will be, and how you will know whether you have been successful.

You will be much more likely to strive to achieve your goals if you write them down. As you progress through college and your career, review your goals from time to time and revise them as your experience grows and your interests change. To get started, answer the following questions:

1. What is my long-term career goal?
2. Where can I get more information about my ideal career?
3. What skills and experience do I need?
4. What classes do I need to take to obtain them?
5. What kinds of jobs (part-time, internship, etc.) can I get to obtain the experience I need?

Informal Assessment

Informal assessment involves gathering information from observations, reports from instructors and supervisors, school and work records, personal interviews and conferences, and computer programs. These assessment methods provide you with information about your current interests, attitudes, and feelings—all of which have a bearing on employability and promotability. Informal assessment instruments include informational interviews, individual and group discussions, and job shadowing.

Skills Assessment

Many student-athletes tend to believe that they have few marketable skills, especially if they have limited experience. You need to remember, however, that your skills come from many sources. You may have developed special abilities in classes, workshops, informal jobs, volunteer work, and even hobbies.

Think of examples of how you have used your skills. You'll need this information as you write your résumé and when you prepare for job interviews. Develop at least two or three brief stories describing how you have used each skill. Begin by analyzing an achievement you are proud of. Break it down into the skills that you used. Include the problem, the action you took, and the result. Use numbers to quantify your accomplishments. For example,

Membership was falling in my student organization. As membership chair, I developed a special recruiting campaign and sought help from the faculty. Through class announcements, a reception with an off-campus professional speaker, and a special dues package, I helped increase our membership by 40 percent and raised an additional $200 in dues revenue.

Three Types of Skills

The three types of skills employers look for are: transferable, personal, and specific.

Transferable skills are those that are used in a variety of jobs and can be transferred from one job to another. Often called "universal" skills, they relate to job performance; employers usually hire applicants based on these. Therefore, it is important to know what transferable skills you have. If you are changing careers or occupations, you must know what skills you can transfer to your new occupation or career.

Personal skills are those you use to function in a job setting. They demonstrate how you act and communicate with others. Sometimes they are called personal traits. *Traits* are qualities used to describe you. These skills are good to mention when an employer asks, "Why should I hire you?" Workers are usually fired because of poor personal skills.

Specific skills are those used to do a specific type of work. They are required for a particular job but cannot be easily transferred from one type of occupation to another. Two examples are operating a crane and programming a computer. Specific or job-related skills usually require some training or experience and are often used to screen applicants.

Skills Employers Look For

Certain transferable and personal skills are needed for entry-level professional occupations. These are occupations that are filled with college graduates and would start at a beginning salary level. These jobs also have room for advancement within the company. Listed here are transferable and personal skills that employers believe are important in entry-level occupations. If you are a college graduate, or soon will be, you may want to go through this list and check the skills that you possess.

Chapter 2   Conducting Your Personal Assessment and Exploring Career Options

Transferable Skills   *Personal Skills*

_____ Leadership   _____ Fast Learner
_____ Writing   _____ Intelligent
_____ Critical Thinking   _____ Mature
_____ Math Skills   _____ Tactful
_____ Anticipate Problems   _____ Assertive
_____ Communication   _____ Precise
_____ Interpersonal Skills   _____ Interest in Work
_____ Decision Making   _____ Open Minded
_____ Listening   _____ Positive Attitude
_____ Verbal Skills   _____ Good Appearance
_____ Organize Information   _____ Self-presentation
_____ Problem Solving   _____ Outgoing
_____ Analysis   _____ Self-promoting
_____ Ability to Delegate   _____ Creative
_____ Research   _____ Motivated

The following list ranks the top ten transferable and personal skills that employers seek when filling entry-level positions.

Transferable Skills   *Personal Skills*

1. Communication   Tactful
2. Writing   Assertive
3. Verbal Skills   Outgoing
4. Interpersonal Skills   Fast Learner
5. Problem Solving   Positive Attitude
6. Analysis   Interest in Work
7. Listening   Good Appearance
8. Math Skills   Motivated
9. Organize Information   Self-promoting
10. Research   Good Self-presentation

SOURCE: *Texas Job Hunter's Guide*

Take a minute or so to go over the skills you checked in the earlier list. You may possess many of these skills, but ask yourself: Which do I really enjoy using the most? After all, you may be able to type 100 words a minute, but do you enjoy typing 100 words a minute? Do you enjoy skills that relate to people or ideas? Or do you prefer those that involve working with things? The closer you can match your work to the skills you enjoy using, the more satisfying your work will be.

Your skills can also assist in your job hunting tasks. Writing skills, for example, are used in creating letters of application and résumés. Verbal skills are used in making interview appointments and, of course, during the interview. Math skills can be used to budget your money during the job search and can help you determine what salary you'll need. Using all these skills effectively should help you.

Values Assessment

Values are those often-intangible aspects of a job that bring satisfaction. Consider the following:

- What is important to you?
- What sacrifices would you be willing to make for a job?
- Would you work for a company that did not share your moral or ethical values?
- Do you want to work in an inner city, a suburb, a small town, or a rural area?
- Would you rather work with people, information, or things?
- How important to you is making a high salary?

As you consider questions such as these, begin to weigh them against one another:

- Would you accept a lower salary so that you could work for an organization that exemplified your ethical standards?
- If you preferred working in a suburb, would you accept an inner-city position that paid a much higher salary?

Work Values Checklist

Think carefully about each of the following work values and place a check next to those that are important to you. After you have checked these items, go back and "double check" the three that you consider most important.

_____ **Achievement:** Being able to set and reach goals.

_____ **Advancement:** Being promoted in predictable steps or moving directly to a higher-level job. Wanting to avoid "dead-end" jobs.

_____ **Adventure:** Taking risks.
_____ **Competence:** Showing others what you are capable of.
_____ **Competition:** Competing with others.
_____ **Creativity and self-expression:** Using your imagination to find new ways to do or try something or use artistic abilities.
_____ **Flexible work schedule:** Choosing your own hours.
_____ **Helping others:** Providing direct services to other people to help them solve problems or improve their well-being in some way.
_____ **High salary:** Earning a large amount of money.
_____ **Independence:** Deciding for yourself what to do and how to do it.
_____ **Intellectual stimulation:** Thinking and reasoning as a large part of your work.
_____ **Leadership:** Having a vision, inspiring others to follow.
_____ **Managing:** Directing, managing, or supervising the activities of others.
_____ **Outdoor work:** Being outdoors a large part of the workday.
_____ **Persuading:** Convincing others to take certain actions.
_____ **Physical work:** Being physically active in your work.
_____ **Power:** Managing others.
_____ **Prestige:** Having status and respect in the community.
_____ **Public attention:** Attracting public notice because of appearance or activity.
_____ **Public contact:** Having day-to-day dealings with the public.
_____ **Recognition:** Being noticed by others in the work setting.
_____ **Research work:** Searching for and discovering new facts, developing ways to apply them.
_____ **Seasonal work:** Being employed only at certain times of the year.
_____ **Security:** Working in a career that is not sensitive to recession or to abrupt changes in technology, government spending, or public tastes. Avoiding seasonal ups and downs.
_____ **Spiritual values:** Having spiritual needs met in your work.
_____ **Travel:** Taking frequent business trips.
_____ **Working with children:** Teaching and otherwise caring for children.
_____ **Working with machines or equipment:** Using machines or equipment.
_____ **Working with your hands:** Using your hands or hand tools.

SOURCE: *Texas Job Hunter's Guide*

Work Values Assessment

What does a job have to be like in order to be satisfying to you? What is important to you may not be important to someone else. Look at the following list of work values. Think generally of any career or job that you would like to have and then rate each value as being very important, moderately important, somewhat important, or not important in terms of your job satisfaction. Place a check (✓) in the column that best represents your choice.

Work Value	Very Important	Moderately Important	Somewhat Important	Not Important
Enjoying pleasant surroundings				
Having my own office				
Working with a group of people				
Working by myself				
Producing a product I can see at the end of the day				
Creating something				
Traveling regularly				
Having flexible work hours				
Being my own boss				
Supervising others				
Earning overtime pay				
Running my own business				
Not working overtime				
Working on projects as a member of a team				
Being supervised by someone I respect				
Having a good benefits package				
Getting a high salary				
Working with little or no supervision				
Working in a large office with my colleagues				
Working independently				
Having a sense of helping society				
Going to lunch at a regular time				
Working for a large organization				
Working in a city				
Having different things to do every day				
Working close to home				
Never having to work on weekends				
Never having to bring work home				

(continued)

Work Value	Very Important	Moderately Important	Somewhat Important	Not Important
Commuting to work Having job security Working with my hands Doing work involving writing Not having pressure on the job				
Being able to work past age 65 Meeting new people regularly Convincing others to do or buy something Having the opportunity for advancement Having the opportunity to change from one job to another within the organization				
Taking vacations Having supportive co-workers Attending social activities after work Working in a pressured environment Having paid holidays				
Attending professional activities Being paid to go to school Developing the skills to move easily from one organization to another Working where unions are allowed Working primarily outdoors				
Working primarily indoors Working where I can use physical skills Working where I usually sit at a desk Working where I primarily use mental skills Working with few immediate but potential long-term rewards				
Working where I can take a project and follow it through over time Doing work that I can complete that day Working in social service Working for the government Working in education				
Working in business Working in a nonsmoking environment Having a window in the area				
Other:				

SOURCE: *University of California at Santa Barbara, Counseling Career Services*

How To Use This Assessment

Now that you have placed a level of importance on a variety of work values, you can compare them with careers in which you are interested. The remainder of this chapter and this book provides guides for you to research your careers. One way to research careers is called informational interviewing. Talk to individuals who are already working in the field you are considering. Ask questions that relate to work values that you ranked "Very Important" and "Moderately Important." If the answers you receive do not correlate with your requirements, you will need to make a decision about the impact that the lack of this value will have on your job satisfaction and success.

Another way to research careers is through the software programs discussed in this chapter. Again, compare those values that are marked very or moderately important to the information that is provided in these computer-assisted software programs. You can narrow your career choices by eliminating those careers that do not match your assessment of important work values.

Your Ideal Job

Another way to discover work values is to create an ideal job. In the next exercise are several incomplete sentences, each followed by several phrases that could complete it. Put a check by each phrase that accurately completes the statement about your ideal job. On the blank lines add ideas of your own. It is essential in this exercise to let your imagination go. This is your ideal job. It has no limits in salary, people with whom you work, or the work itself. This is your chance to dream!

SOURCE: *Texas Job Hunter's Guide*

My ideal job will allow me to:

_____ work on my own.

_____ work inside.

_____ be challenged creatively.

_____ use my skills to the fullest.

_____ see the end product of my work.

_____ work as a member of a team or workgroup.

_____ work outside.

Chapter 2 Conducting Your Personal Assessment and Exploring Career Options

My boss will:

_____ involve me in decision making.

_____ watch my work closely.

_____ be fair.

_____ be a good leader.

_____ be open and honest.

_____ allow me to do my job as I best see fit.

The people I work with will:

_____ be fun to be around.

_____ become good friends.

_____ leave me alone to do my work.

_____ want to work as hard as I do.

_____ be able to work as a team.

_____ be technically skilled.

_____ be great thinkers.

_____ be concerned with community activities.

My ideal job will have:

_____ parking nearby.

_____ an attractive office for me.

_____ a quiet place for me to work.

_____ flexible hours.

_____ public transportation nearby.

_____ a particular physical environment I enjoy (i.e. skyscraper, factory).

My ideal job will provide me with:

_____ at least $ _____ per year.

_____ a chance to advance in the company.

_____ paid vacation time.

_____ extra pay for overtime.

_____ good health benefits.

_____ other benefits (perks, continuing education).

_____

_____

Review your earlier work value assessment. Do these values and your ideal job fit together? Your ideal job should reflect the values you hold. Remember, however, that you may have to make adjustments to get a job in the real world.

Career Assessment

If you've worked this far through the chapter, you've taken the first step in the career development process, self-assessment—clarifying your interests, assessing your values, and determining your skills. To give yourself a better chance of making a satisfying career choice, you are encouraged to use more formal assessment tools that link your personal attributes with occupational choices.

Formal Assessment

Most formal assessment instruments fall into one or more of these: (1) aptitude and ability tests, (2) interest inventories, (3) values assessments, (4) career development assessments, and (5) personality or management style inventories. There are no magic answers to be found in career inventories and tests, but if you are having difficulty determining your interests and values and how they might relate to specific career choices, the following tools, available at most career planning centers, may help you.

SIGI-Plus (see p. 27) is an interactive career guidance program to help you assess your interests, values, and preferred activities and to provide suggestions of careers that should meet your expressed criteria. It provides detailed information on more than 200 careers.

Discover is a multimedia career exploration tool that provides a personalized list of possible occupations and majors based on three inventories of your interests, work-related abilities, and values. The program includes four sections or "halls." Hall 1 includes the three inventories about yourself. Choosing an occupation is the focus of Hall 2. Users are able to view occupations based on inventory results, the world-of-work map, and occupational characteristics or titles. Hall 3 enables users to plan their education by selecting majors, schools, and appropriate financial aid options. Finally, Hall 4 assists users in defining their ideal job and preparing for the job search.

The Campbell Interest and Skill Survey (CISS) is a survey of self-reported interests and skills. Its major purpose is to help individuals understand how their interests and skills fit the occupational world, thereby helping them make better career choices. Before taking the CISS you are required to meet with a counselor. Results are interpreted and discussed in a follow-up appointment.

The Myers-Briggs Type Indicator (MBTI) is utilized to assist individuals as they identify their personality strengths, preferred work environments, communication styles, and career possibilities. While no occupation provides a perfect match between personality and work tasks, this indicator will assist you in making an informed decision. Estimated completion time: one-half hour. Interpretation: two-hour small group workshop.

The Strong Interest Inventory (SII) provides detailed information regarding an individual's career-related and leisure interests. Identified interest patterns are compared to people actively working in a wide variety of occupations. The power of the SII rests on two assumptions: (1) Activities typical of an occupation are reflected in the interests of the people who are employed in it, and (2) those who have similar patterns of interests will be satisfied in an occupation if they have compatible values and the necessary knowledge and abilities. Estimated completion time: one-half hour. Interpretation: two-hour small group workshop.

There are literally hundreds of formal assessments that could be used in the workplace. As you consider the array of career assessments keep two basic points in mind: (1) Identify those instruments/methods that meet your information needs, and (2) be aware that a fee may be charged for the use of some tests. Computerized tests may give instant scoring. Those done with paper and pencil may be self-scored, and many can be sent out for machine scoring by the test publisher.

Although the latter are more expensive, the test interpretation booklets and summary reports available from the test publisher may be very helpful and timesaving.

SIGI Plus

SIGI Plus, pronounced "siggy plus," is an acronym for *System of Interactive Guidance and Information PLUS*. It is a computer-aided career-planning program, but no computer skills are necessary to use the program. SIGI is helpful during any stage of the career-planning process, because it can help assess interests, values, and activities and can provide a list of related career options. The program includes the following sections.

1. **Introduction.** Recommends a pathway through the program based on one of the following situations:
   - You do not have any career ideas
   - You are trying to decide on a major
   - You have a career in mind, but you would like to know more about it
   - You want to find a career to utilize the skills and experience you already have
   - You are just curious about SIGI Plus
   - None of the above
2. **Self-Assessment.** Helps identify interests, values, and activities you enjoy and in which you excel. SIGI matches these with career choices.

Interests

arts and humanities	social and behavioral sciences
business	sports and physical education
health	trades and technologies
science and math	

Values

advancement	easy commute
contribution to society	independence
security	flexible hours
challenge	leadership
high income	on-the-job learning
pleasant co-workers	leisure
prestige	variety

Activities

working with people	communicating
working with hands or equipment	working with math
organizing information	special events

(continued)

SIGI Plus (continued)

3. **Search.** Presents a list of occupations based on the features you choose. You may view a list of occupations matched to one or more of the following categories:

   - interests
   - actitvies
   - college major
   - values
   - required education/training

   You are able to cross-reference the previous features. You may also ask for a list based on features you would prefer to avoid including:

   - outdoor work
   - mathematics
   - sedentary work
   - writing
   - public speaking
   - keen competition for jobs

   In addition, the search section will tell you why a particular occupation was not chosen.

4. **Information.** Compares any two occupations you choose using definitions and descriptions, education, training and other requirements, potential incomes, personal satisfactions, advancement possibilities, and national employment outlooks.

5. **Skills.** Describes skills needed for any occupation you specify and allows you to rate yourself on these skills.

6. **Preparing.** Illustrates preparation paths for any occupation, including training or college education and helpful experience. College education includes courses, course descriptions, and work tasks. This section also considers time, money, difficulty, and motivation.

7. **Coping.** Contains advice on subjects associated with preparing for and holding a job. Subject areas include obtaining college credit, managing time, finding money, relocating, arranging child care, and managing common worries. Altogether, there are 27 subjects.

8. **Deciding.** Allows you to consider the rewards and chances you would have in a chosen occupation. You can measure rewards by examining how well the occupation meets your values, satisfies your interests, and includes activities you enjoy. You evaluate your chances by seeing if you have the necessary skills, can complete the required preparation, and can find a position. This section allows you to evaluate as many as three occupations at one time.

9. **Next Steps.** Presents a variety of short-term goals. SIGI Plus will help plan your first steps for any goals you specify as potentially difficult.

Goals

- getting more education or training
- developing new skills
- proving you can do the work
- building a network of contacts
- writing a résumé
- dealing with obstacles

Informational Interviewing and Career Shadowing

Informational interviewing and career shadowing are two ways to obtain career information that cannot be found in a book. Informational interviewing means sitting down with a professional to ask questions about the career he or she is pursuing. Career shadowing means following a professional on the job in order to observe his or her day-to-day routine. Informational interviewing and career shadowing provide an excellent opportunity to further explore career fields that interest you. You can see if you would enjoy the job and if you have or will be able to acquire the necessary skills. Later, these methods will aid in the job search process. You'll be better able to convey your understanding of what a particular job encompasses and why your skills make you the best applicant for the job. In order to conduct an informational interview or shadow someone, follow these steps:

1. Find someone to interview or shadow.

Use contacts including acquaintances, friends, relatives, professors, teaching assistants, coaches, college advisors, academic supervisors, and career planning and placement assistants. Check the Yellow Pages for other candidates for informational interviewing.

2. Schedule an appointment.

Introduce yourself and mention the person who referred you. In the case of an interview, offer to meet for 15-20 minutes in the person's office or for lunch. If a phone interview would be more convenient for the interviewee, offer to call back when he or she has some free time. In many cases, the interview will last longer than 20 minutes. Most people enjoy discussing their professions. Therefore, give yourself plenty of extra time. Shadowing also requires an appointment, but try to schedule an hour or more. Also, try to meet with at least two people in each of your areas of interest. (For more details on scheduling an appointment see "How To Set up an Informational Interview" later in this chapter.)

3. Prepare for the interview.

Conduct some basic research. Know, in general, what people in the position do. Also, research the company. Use material from the career center or library to find out everything you can *before* the interview. Develop a list of good questions, especially for information interviews—questions that you were unable to answer from your material. Examples are listed at the end of this section.

4. Keep the appointment.

Dress appropriately. Be sure the professional understands you are there for opinions and advice, not a job. At a later date you may be able to ask for job opening referrals or obtain help networking in the field, but do not use the informational interview as an opportunity to push your résumé on someone. Give a very brief background history when you introduce yourself. Take notes. Be sure to thank the person for his or her time and information. Ask the person to recommend you to anyone else in the field who might be willing to discuss his or her career (be sure to get names, addresses, and phone numbers).

5. Follow-up.

Write a thank-you letter within a week. If the meeting was positive, stay in contact. If a referral turned out well, send a thank-you letter to the person who made the referral. Also, send another thank-you if you later take a position in the field.

Sample Questions

Here are some questions that might be used in an informational interview:

Job Description

How does your department or function serve the organization?
What is a typical day like in your position? Month? Year?
What percent of each day do you spend on each task?
How much freedom do you have? Variety?
What opportunities do you have to influence people? Direct policies?
What kind of recognition do you get from your work?
What are the most satisfying aspects of your work? The most frustrating?
What constraints, such as financial, legal, supervisory, policy, and consumer-related, affect you in your work?
What hours do you normally work? How about travel?

Background

What education, training, or licenses do you need?
What is the effect of a degree or training beyond the basic requirements?
What is required or helpful for advancement?

What other parts of your background, such as travel, extracurricular activities, and internships have been helpful?

Advancement

How did you reach this position? Is this a typical path?

What entry-level jobs are appropriate for this position now?

What criteria should be considered when choosing an entry-level job?

What trends or developments will affect the career of someone entering the field now?

What are the possibilities for advancement in your company? In your field?

Informational Interview Suggestions

Remember, an informational interview is not a job interview. It has a very different focus and purpose. You are exploring alternatives and talking informally with someone rather than trying to sell yourself. You are the interviewer rather than the interviewee. When you call to set up an informational interview, make sure you:

- Give your name, affiliation (your school, organization, etc.), and the name of the person who suggested you call (if applicable).
- Explain the purpose of your visit—to learn about the field in order to help you explore various career options. Set a time limit of 15–20 minutes.
- Ask to meet in person so you can see the work environment. Remember to be flexible. You might have to work around the person's busy schedule.
- Get complete directions to the place of business, and leave your phone number in case the interview must be rescheduled. Also, be sure to get the person's name and title so you know whom to ask for.
- Prepare the questions you want to consider asking. However, more important than a prepared script is the ability to be flexible and follow through on topics that come up during the interview.

There are many benefits to conducting informational interviews to explore career options. They provide you the opportunity to meet people in your field of interest in a low-risk, nonthreatening situation. It helps to have an insider's view of the career you are considering. As you gather information tailored to your specific questions, you'll be practicing your interviewing skills. You'll also make contacts, which may lead to future job leads, networking opportunities, and possible mentor relationships. It helps to have an advocate already in your area of interest when you are job hunting.

Informational Interviewing—A Worksheet

Answer these questions, to prepare yourself for each informational interview that you will be seeking:

1. Field of work I am considering.
2. Local organizations I have identified where I may seek informational interviews.
3. Other individuals with whom I plan to seek informational interviews.

The following categories represent possible areas of questioning for the informational interview. For each of the three (field of work, personal responses, and specific job), there are several topics. For at least three of the topics in each category, write the particular question you would like to ask.

Example:

1. Where employed—"Does your company have branches in Colorado?"
2. Problems of job—"How much pressure is there in news reporting?"

<u>Questions I want to ask in the informational interview</u>

Field of Work

1. Credential requirements _____
2. Nature of work _____
3. Where employed _____
4. Earnings _____
5. Advancement potential _____
6. Related fields of work _____

Personal Responses

1. Rewards of the job _____
2. Problems of the job _____
3. Skills developed _____
4. Advancement potential _____
5. Uncertainties of the job _____
6. Greatest disappointments _____
7. Greatest surprises _____

Specific Job

1. Major responsibilities _____
2. Key problems _____
3. Criteria for hiring _____
4. Academic requirements _____
5. Nature of work _____
6. Resources available to do job _____
7. Training opportunities _____

How To Set up an Informational Interview

1. Get the telephone number of the organization where you would like to do an informational interview. Call and ask for the name of the person with whom you would like to speak ("Who is the head of the _____ department?")

2. Telephone the person you want to talk with. If he or she is not available, ask for someone else who works in that department.

3. Say to this person: "I am interested in the kind of work that your organization does and would like to know more about it. I am not looking for a job. Instead, I need information and possible advice about how to get into this field and what the work is like. Could I meet with you at your convenience to ask a few questions?"

4. If this person cannot meet with you, ask him/her if someone else in the department would be willing to talk with you.

5. **Note:** You can also request informational interviews in person. The more informal the organization (smaller firms tend to be less formal), the more likely you might get an informational interview on a walk-in basis.

Additional Guidelines

Schedule your first informational interviews with people who are easy to contact, either because you know them or because they are easily available. This will help you become accustomed to the process, so that you can approach less familiar people later. You'll gain much confidence after completing several interviews, and that's a great benefit regardless of the student or desired field of work.

Do not assume that people will take a lot of time to talk with you. Be respectful of their time. Ask only those questions which are most important to you. If someone resists a particular question you have asked, move on to another without pursuing the first one. Listen attentively. Do not interrupt your interviewee even when a different question occurs to you while he or she is talking.

Before leaving an interview, ask for references to other people and/or materials that can extend your search for relevant information. You may even hear about some job openings while you are informational interviewing, because the word-of-mouth network is always strong. But remember, your main purpose is to gain valuable information insights that will help you to decide among future career or job possibilities.

▲ Conclusion and Activity

You have now been provided with a variety of resources that will assist you in completing a full-scale self-assessment. The ball is in your court to determine the next move.

Visit your academic or career center advisor to see if your college or university has any computer-assisted career guidance programs. If so, spend some quality time utilizing these tools. Second, complete the Work Values Assessment and Your Ideal Job exercise found in this chapter. Equipped with this information, visit your career center or library again. Find information regarding the careers in which you are interested and then compare them to your values and ideal job assessments. Eliminate those jobs that do not correspond with your wants and needs. Save the information on those jobs that you are still considering; you will use it in the next chapter when writing your job search marketing plan.

Chapter 3
Assessing Your Marketability and Planning a Job Search Strategy

INTRODUCTION

Determining your job search plan is like setting a game plan. Rather than listing who will compete in which events or what plays will be called during the game, however, you are developing a detailed plan of how you will attain your ideal job. Just as developing a game plan takes weeks of practice and training, developing an effective job search plan requires a lot of time and research.

This chapter provides you with the tools you need to prepare such a job search plan. It also offers you a timeline for your college career, indicating some tasks you should accomplish each year to make progress toward your ultimate job search as graduation nears. Developing a job search plan will give you direction and focus so that you perform at your very best.

Résumé Worksheet

Employers often decide whether or not to interview someone by looking at a résumé. We'll discuss résumés more in the next chapter; but for now, a résumé worksheet is the first step in evaluating your marketability. The worksheet will help identify any areas in need of improvement. Also, since a résumé may be necessary for obtaining a summer job, this worksheet will serve as a good rough draft.

Now you are ready to evaluate your résumé. Think about the answers to the following questions.

- Is your major related to your career goal?
- Are you holding leadership positions in any student organizations?
- Do you have any career-related experience?
- Are there any time gaps in your résumé?

If the answers do not satisfy you, do not worry. By evaluating your résumé early, you have time to make any necessary improvements (participating in leadership opportunities, gaining-career related experience, joining organizations, taking relevant courses, etc.)

Four-Year Career Planning

Freshman Year: Orientation/Adapting

Learn how to succeed:

- Identify interests and explore potential majors.
- Enlist the aid of faculty, advisors, counselors, administrators, and friends. Review various career and business publications. Use exercises, projects, psychological tests, and other methods to determine your career interests.
- Attend classes and keep your grades as high as you can to be eligible for the college or department of your choice.
- Do the planning and goal setting required to be ready for your academic progress—check at thirty credit hours.
- Create your own personal career action plan and job search log. Insert your career planning exercises, notes on short-term and long-term career goals, and other notes regarding your progress into your log on a regular basis.

Résumé Worksheet

Education
college   city/state   major/minor   GPA   degree   graduation date
_____

high school   city/state   GPA   graduation date
_____

Work Experience
dates   company   city/state   title   responsibilities   skills used
_____
_____
_____

Community Service/Membership/Offices held in civic, professional, social, service, or educational organizations
dates   organization   office   responsibilities   skills used
_____
_____
_____
_____

Academic, professional, and civic awards and honors
date   award or honor
_____
_____
_____

Athletic participation, awards and honors
date   team   award or honor
_____
_____
_____

Certificates, special skills, or accomplishments
_____
_____

- Include in your plan the answers to the following four key questions:
    1. What do I want to do?
    2. What can I do?
    3. What do I need to do to develop myself further?
    4. How can I get the job I want after graduation?

Become involved in college as preparation for life-long learning:

- Explore campus activities and student organizations
- Volunteer for community service while gaining interpersonal and public relations skills.

Self-Assessment:

- Think about and relate your academic choices to career options.
- Collect, analyze, and evaluate information about yourself to aid you in obtaining a career position consistent with your personality, abilities, aptitudes, values, interests, academic training, past work, and life experiences.
- Visit the career resource center to learn about the services it provides.
- Attend a career day, career expo, and other career fairs to consider career options and types of jobs available.
- Develop your résumé for a summer job.

Summer:

- Find work related to your interests to gain work experience and to develop a strong work ethic.
- Develop awareness of your skills, interests, and values.
- Develop and enhance your ability to interact with people and to function in a work environment.

<u>*Sophomore Year: Self-Assessment/Exploration*</u>

Self-assessment:

- Evaluate your strengths, skills, values, and interests
- If undecided about a major or career, visit the career resource specialist and attend mini-courses on choosing a major or choosing a

career. It can also be helpful to visit your student counseling office, which may provide career counseling.
- Discuss career ideas with counselors, friends, faculty, and family.
- Update your résumé, make contact lists, prepare cover letter formats, and investigate various job-search strategies.

Become a student of possibilities:

- Attend a career expo, career day, and/or other career fairs to talk to company representatives about the qualities and qualifications they seek in employees.
- Involve yourself in career-related experiences: an internship, a cooperative education program, or volunteer work.
- Select courses to enhance your personal and career goals.
- Join campus organizations and develop leadership skills on and off the playing field.
- Develop a file of information about specific career alternatives and narrow your potential career options. Develop an array of information about specific careers. Collect information about types of opportunities in managerial, technical, and professional career areas.
- Accumulate and analyze information about the world of work, office politics, corporate culture, and work force diversity.
- Write the answers to the following three key questions and place them in your career action plan file:
    1. What do I have to offer an employer?
    2. Who needs what I have to offer?
    3. How do I make them want me?

Start setting goals:

- Think about how you want your education to serve you. Consider what you will do in the future, where you will accomplish this, and how you will get there.
- Select a major by the end of your sophomore year.
- Prepare for academic progress checks at 45 and 60 credit hours.
- Since the NCAA now allows scholarship student-athletes to be employed during the academic year, decide whether would you be interested in or have the time to hold down a part-time job.

Summer:

- Get a summer job and continue to earn money for expenses. Build a good work reputation and relationships, and acquire work references.
- Develop career-related skills and maturity as well as computer skills.
- Gain knowledge about the workplace and what it takes to achieve success.

Junior Year: Decision Making/Goal Setting

Set career goals:

- Develop career goals and a strategy plan.
- Develop alternative career plans.
- Determine and fulfill any academic requirements needed for graduation and career field. Strive for good grades!
- Test your qualifications for work in your field of interest.

Become knowledgeable about a job search:

- Attend workshops on résumé writing, cover letters, interview skills, job search strategies, and researching occupations and companies.
- Get hands-on experience (reality testing) via an internship, clinical or field experience, or a volunteer position. Utilize the career network for shadowing and mentoring opportunities
- Identify companies that interest you.
- Attend career fairs and career day, visiting companies on your list.
- Considering graduate school? Take the necessary exams.
- Review and update your résumé and job correspondence. Analyze the skills you've acquired through participation in college athletics and experience in work or volunteer positions. List those skills on your résumé.
- Practice interview skills.
- For assistance with career planning, visit the career center; check with career planning and placement services for on-campus interview schedules and employer listings.

Network:

- Know faculty, counselors, career advisors, administrators, and professionals in your area of interest.

- Be active in civic, charitable, community, or social organizations.

Summer:

- Get a summer job in your chosen field. Continue to earn money to cover expenses and enhance your marketable skills for jobs after graduation.
- Continue developing career-related and computer skills.
- Gain more knowledge of the workplace.
- Compile an inventory of interests and qualifications during your Junior Year.

Senior Year: Job Search/Implementation

- Kick your job-search campaign into high gear: Commit yourself to a thorough search. Schedule interviews on campus and on site with as many employers as possible. Conduct your own job search; don't rely on or restrict yourself to campus interviews.
- Use your network to learn about opportunities for references and for support.
- Discuss career opportunities with faculty, friends, counselors, acquaintances, network contacts, and so on.
- Identify and research companies/organizations that interest you and those that are actively recruiting job candidates in your major.
- Register for on-campus interviews and update your résumé.
- Attend career fairs to meet employers and set up interviews.
- Pursue leadership roles in campus organizations.
- Keep your career-planning log updated with contacts, interview results, and assessments of how you performed during job interviews.
- Consider and choose from among the various job offers you receive.
- Accept the job that best fits your career goals and professional needs.
- Develop a checklist of areas to address when making your transition from college into the work environment.
- Find a mentor or join a support group to help you adjust to your new work environment. Learn the corporate culture and office policies.
- Perform efficiently. Be an effective team member.

Career Planning Advice

The Job Search: A Nine-Step Approach

When entering the job market, you should think of yourself as a salesperson. You say you aren't interested in sales? Well, the product that you are selling shouldn't be a tough sale. After all, you know more about this product than anyone else does. You are selling *yourself*!

Before selling yourself, you must first understand all the positive characteristics that you have to offer. In other words, why would someone want to hire you? Make a list of your accomplishments as well as a list of the things you want from a job, such as salary and job location. You must then identify what companies and industries would be willing to make an investment in a product like you. Then, you must market your product with résumés and cover letters in order to obtain job interviews. Finally, the job interview is your opportunity to make and close the sale. This is the most important sale you will make, so invest the time and energy needed to promote this valuable product—YOU!

1. Define the Product
   - My academic knowledge bases
   - My career skills with examples
   - Motivation and career values
   - How to describe my personality
   - Locations I want
   - Salary I want

2. Identify the Market
   - Industries
   - Job functions
   - Location

3. Manage an Independent Job Search
   - Devote hours to job search
   - Commit to goals
   - Plan times of intense effort

4. Locate Possible Employers
   - Career fairs
   - Career library
   - Newspapers

- On-campus recruiters
- Job postings
- Former students
- Professors

5. Request Interviews
   - Write letters
   - Follow-up calls
   - Campus interviews

6. Advertise (carefully study job announcements)
   - Résumés
   - Cover letters
   - Portfolio of work

7. Make Sales Presentation
   - Practice: Five reasons to hire me
   - Interview

8. Close the Sale
   - Ask for the job
   - Ask for referrals

9. Follow-up
   - Send professional letters—thank you letters to those who helped you, interviewed you, those you networked with, etc.

Job Search Strategies

The most important step in the job search is identifying *what kind of job you want* and *what you have to offer* the employer. To determine that you need to:

SOURCE: *NCAA Life Skills Career Development Notebook*

- Identify your interests, skills, experience, knowledge, and attributes (include those skills and attributes gained through participation in athletics).
- Identify and research occupations of interest. This can be accomplished through books, classes, information interviews, and experimental learning opportunities (summer jobs, internships, and practicums).
- Decide on the work environment you would most prefer. You can consider the following sectors: business, education, government, social service, professions, and private enterprise.

You should then be able to write your goal statement, including the skills you want to use, the kind of work you want to do, and the work environment you would like to be in. Use the following format:

"I want to do _____
(tasks and responsibilities)

using _____
(skills, knowledge, experience)

in _____."
(setting)

Learn as much as you can about the work you are interested in. Find out what the work involves, what salary you might expect, and the training and education required. Talk with people employed in your area of interest, read job descriptions and professional journals.

At this point you can prepare one or more versions of your résumé, (see chapter 4). Once you have assessed your skills and experiences and have learned about the requirements of the position, you can tailor your résumé to the position. You also need to prepare an effective cover letter (see Chapter 7), which highlights your qualifications for the company and the position.

Think about who would be interested in hiring you. Possible employers can be identified through the following information resources: informational interviews, news media, Yellow Pages of the phone book, Chamber of Commerce listings, word of mouth, professional journals, placement office and department postings, the library reference room, specialized directories, special interest groups, your Alumni Association, help-wanted ads, and contacts made through athletic participation.

Next, gather information about employers, their products, services, positions available, and hiring needs. This can be accomplished through the career center library, the Internet, and so forth.

Narrow down your list of possible job prospects and contact potential employers about a job. The objective of the initial contact is to obtain an interview. Your résumé and cover letter will introduce you. The interview will provide the opportunity for you to speak to the employer and expand on the information provided in the résumé and cover letter.

Follow up your résumé and cover letters to companies of particular interest, even when you have gotten no response. Be persistent, but remain polite. When you get an appointment, prepare for the interview, and write a thank-you letter following the interview (see Chapter 9).

Assess your progress regularly and make changes where feasible. Maintain careful records of contacts made, the action taken, and the follow-up made regarding each contact. Make copies of all information sent to possible employers and make notes of all telephone conversations. Continue to increase your network of contacts.

Job Search Marketing Plan

It is now time to prepare a marketing plan for your job search. A job search marketing plan is like a road map steering you toward your ultimate goal of finding a satisfying career. After all, if you don't know where you are going, it is really hard to get there. Think of your marketing plan as if it were your athletic game plan. You know what you want—a victory. Now you need to outline how you will attain that victory. Included in this game plan are steps you will take to learn more about yourself, more about the industry and companies you are interested in, and how you will go about making a successful match between these two entities.

This marketing plan outlines three major steps:

1. Prepare yourself
2. Research the market
3. Move into the marketplace to win

You should know or identify the following key points about yourself:

Step 1: You are the focus

Skills/talent inventory	Potential salary range
Personality characteristics	Career focus to consider
Geographical preferences	Career objective statement
Special knowledge you have	Qualifications summary
Recent education, seminars attended	Experience/ education to support career objective
Continuing experience levels	Credentials in order
Expectations for workplace	College transcripts ready
Management style that works best for you	References identified: personal/professional

Organizational goals with which you can identify

Ethics/values you expect to find in the workplace

Awards/honors

Step 2: Research is the focus

Research companies you like

Research cities you like

Identify fifteen to twenty companies you like

Identify peers in the field

Clarify the individual most likely to need your skill, talent, and education

Identify job acceptance criteria

Build résumé to be printed

Develop cover letter, network, target market

Develop questions for interviews

Gather data and chart information for actual job search

You should do the following:

Step 3: Marketplace is the focus

Your goal should be to see from four to five people weekly if you are conducting a part-time search. Keep a calendar or journal to record your job search activities and monitor your progress.

Some Key Points to Remember

We all have unique talents, experiences, and skills that set us apart. Know what is special about you and use it to sell yourself.

Your ideal job should be a comfortable mix of what you want to do, where you want to do it, how much you want to get paid to do it, and the environment in which you want to do it.

Most jobs aren't found in the paper or on the Web. Remember this as you broaden your marketplace search.

Organizing and Conducting a Job Search

Locating a job is like playing detective: You follow many false clues, and progress is difficult to judge. Few of us easily find jobs because it is something we do only a few times in our lives.

Only *you* can decide what you should be doing. It is madness not to put time and energy into finding a fulfilling, satisfying career, when your job consumes half of your waking hours! The idea of being handed a dream job on a silver platter is one of the hardest myths to let go.

Organization

How you run your job search is a reflection of the type of worker you'll be. Employers will notice if you're running a well-planned, effective search. So stay organized; it is easy to lose momentum if you're not organized.

Dedication

Allow time for things to happen. Three months is the average time it takes someone to find an entry-level position. But persistence and a tireless work ethic result in career victory. Force yourself to do things you'd rather not do (such as the hard, but necessary tasks: research, interview preparation, follow-up, etc.).

Seeking a career position takes time and energy, but you won't get that job unless you approach the right person (the decision-maker, not the personnel or human resources department) with a well-thought-out campaign.

Where To Begin

Prepare your résumé, curriculum transcripts, employment proposal, background letter, or video presentation so you'll be able to talk about yourself.

Ask friends, coaches, professors, and business contacts for leads. Everyone has his or her own network of friends that might be able to help you find the job you're looking for!

Use contacts within the company to help you find your job; they'll be able to direct you past the human resources department to the decision maker. Everything happens through people, not paper. Carefully avoid personnel or human resources departments.

Mailing a résumé should be a last resort. The best résumé is the one you take to the decision maker after you've talked to him or her personally.

Second is the one that someone carries in for you (and says that you walk on water!).

Third is the one *you* carry in yourself. If you're told to mail it, reply that you'll be on that side of town and want to bring it by personally (you'll be less likely to be forgotten).

Last would be mailing a résumé complete with a cover letter, just as they told you to do. This résumé will land in a stack with everyone else's, usually on a clerk's desk!

Research the Prospective Employer

Investigate companies and positions.

Find out everything you can about your target companies so that you can intelligently discuss their business. Research is an important aspect of any job search. This can be accomplished through the career center and the Internet. Also check the library business section. Look in stock buyer's guides such as *Standard & Poor's* or *Moody's* and trade publications. Employers can be turned off by a candidate who does not know the elementary facts about company operations. Also keep in mind that you are most likely to be hired by your "clone"—someone who is like you—so you need to know yourself and know the company.

Job Hunting Hints

An important part of being able to find work is learning where to hunt for jobs. Information on openings can come from a variety of sources, such as employment agencies, newspapers, and friends. Many people keep their search for a job too narrow; they do not look in enough places. While searching for work you should try as many job-search methods as possible. This section of the book will help you identify the job hunting methods and resources that have proven to be successful for others.

Where To Look for Openings

For many people, the search for job openings begins with the newspaper. After this, most people do not know where to look. However, two methods for finding openings are more successful: talking with friends and relatives, and applying directly to the employer. A list of successful ways in which employment has been found are listed here.

How People Find Job Openings

1. Friends and relatives
2. Applying directly to employers

3. Newspaper want ads
4. Working for temporary employment services
5. Public and private employment agencies
6. Government programs
7. Labor unions
8. School placement programs
9. Asking former teachers
10. Civil Service tests
11. Answering ads in professional or trade journals
12. Placing ads in newspapers

Hidden Job Market

Before you start your search for open jobs, it is important that you learn about the hidden job market—those vacancies that are never made known to the public. Some experts estimate that 80 percent of all openings are hidden from the public. Two types of jobs can be found in the hidden market. The first are those that are not advertised in newspapers or listed with employment agencies. These openings are

---

HOW PEOPLE FIND JOBS

Informal Job-Seeking Methods
- Direct contact with employers
- Networking: identification of potential employers through family, friends, and acquaintances.

Want Ads
- Answering ads in the newspaper
- Answering ads in professional or trade journals
- Placing ads citing job desired

Agencies
- Public employment agencies
- Private employment agencies

Other Methods
- Civil Service tests and offices
- School placement offices

posted "inside" the business and are often filled by current employees. In many cases these jobs are filled by friends, relatives, or acquaintances of employees. Because of the way these jobs are filled, you must apply directly to the employer or ask friends and relatives about such openings.

Jobs can also be hidden from the employer. This is the second type of job in the hidden market. A business, for example, may have a problem getting its work finished on time. You, however, know a faster, cheaper, or safer way of completing the work. You can present your plan to the employer and perhaps create a new position for yourself. The new job was hidden from the employer.

FOUR STAGES OF A JOB OPENING

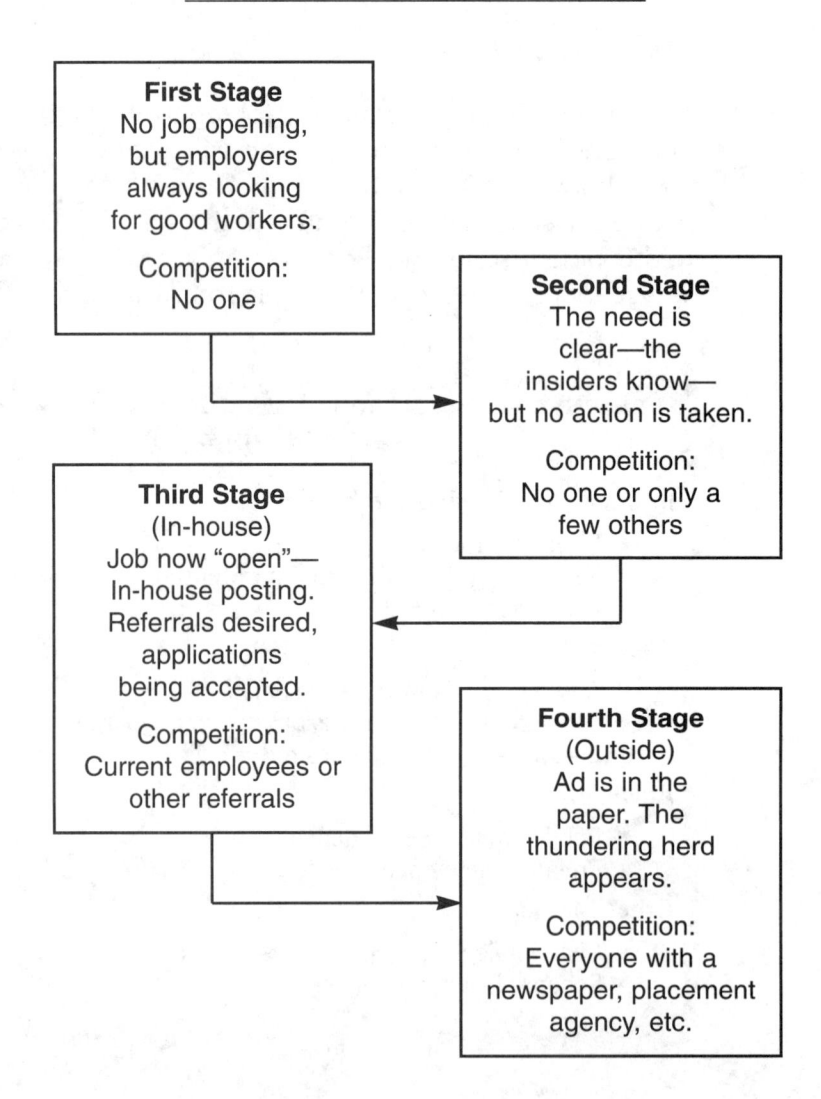

First Stage
No job opening, but employers always looking for good workers.

Competition: No one

Second Stage
The need is clear—the insiders know—but no action is taken.

Competition: No one or only a few others

Third Stage
(In-house)
Job now "open"—In-house posting. Referrals desired, applications being accepted.

Competition: Current employees or other referrals

Fourth Stage
(Outside)
Ad is in the paper. The thundering herd appears.

Competition: Everyone with a newspaper, placement agency, etc.

Your game plan for each of these stages should be as follows:

First Stage: "Create" a need for you and your services. Sell the company on what you can do to make them money or save them money.

Second Stage: Work with the insiders to create that need—they know the business and you know yourself. Form a partnership to sell a "win-win" situation to the employer.

Third Stage: Use your inside contacts to learn about the company and the position. Tailor your cover letter and résumé to highlight how you are the best candidate for the job.

Fourth Stage: Stand out from the crowd with an eye-catching and error-free cover letter and résumé and exceptional interviewing skills.

Employers Look for Specific Traits

Can you set yourself apart from other job candidates? Employers are looking for certain intangible assets. According to Martin Yate, in his book *Knock 'em Dead*, there are twenty universally admired key traits that fall into one of four profiles: personal profile, professional profile, achievement profile, and business profile. These traits are your passport to success in any interview. Use them as a reference to customize your answers to tough questions.

Personal Profile

- Drive: desire to get things done, goal-oriented
- Motivation: enthusiasm and a willingness to ask questions
- Communication skills: the ability to talk and write effectively to people at all levels
- Chemistry: personality and attitude match with the corporate culture, a team player
- Energy: extra effort given to all endeavors, big or small
- Determination: not backing off when faced with tough situations
- Confidence: poise, not easily intimidated nor overly familiar

Professional Profile

- Reliability: can be counted on to get the job done
- Integrity: doing what is morally right

- Pride: feeling good about a job well done
- Dedication: doing whatever it takes to see a project through to completion
- Analytical skills: not jumping at the first solution to a problem
- Listening skills: ability to comprehend and provide insightful feedback

Achievement Profile

- Money saved: reducing company expenses through efficiency and skills
- Time saved: saving the company money through wise use of time
- Money earned: ability to generate revenue for the company

Business Profile

- Efficiency: making good use of time, effort, resources, and money
- Economy: sensitivity to unnecessary overspending
- Procedures: following the chain of command and rules of the company
- Profit: ability to increase the company's earnings

Building these key traits into your answers to interviewers' questions will help you win a job and set the stage for career growth.

Preparing for an Interview

You're excited about an upcoming interview. Everything you have heard about the job, including salary, benefits, hours, and location, sounds ideal. Best of all, you know that you are well qualified for the position. And so, with boundless confidence, you go in, give it your all, and . . . get a rejection letter!

Obviously, the interview did not go as well as it could have. Your qualifications were right, but so were those of other applicants interviewed. Perhaps the one who got the job had greater self-confidence or answered tough questions with greater ease.

When qualifications are equal, you want to stand out as being the best interviewee. Being well prepared for an interview can give you an edge over the competition. There are several things you can do to help prepare for an interview: (1) Research the position, company, and field for which you will interview; (2) perform mock interviews with friends, videotaping them for review; (3) attend an interview skills workshop; (4) when arranging an interview, ask for clear directions and parking instructions; (5) arrive at the interview early; and (6) come prepared with your resumés, reference page, a pen, and paper.

Have you ever been told, " Send me your résumé" or "I don't have time to see you" or "We are not hiring at this time"? Although these phrases seem like brush-off lines, often they are disguised opportunities to get yourself a job offer. Handled properly, almost any objection can lead to interviews.

The following are responses to objections that can be personalized to your character:

Objection: "Why don't you send me a résumé?"
(Danger here. The employer may be genuinely interested in seeing your résumé as a first step in the interview process, or it may be a polite way of getting you off the phone.)

Response: "Of course, Mr. Smith. Would you give me your exact title and full address? [Pause] Thank you. So that I can be sure that my qualifications fit your needs, what skills are you looking for in this position?"
(Answering in this fashion will open up the conversation and allow you to use the information given to draw attention to your specific skills on your résumé.)

Objection: "I don't have time to see you."
(Try to coordinate with the employer to schedule a time that is convenient for him or her to discuss the job.)

Response: "Since you are currently busy, what is the best time of day for you? First thing in the morning, or is the afternoon a quieter time?"
(By presuming the invitation for a meeting, it is harder for the employer to object.)

Objection: "We are not hiring at this time."
(Chances of getting an interview with this particular company may be slim.)

Response: "Who else in the company might need someone with my qualifications?" or "When do you anticipate an opening in your company?"

Employer's Expectations

Employers have expectations of their ideal candidate. It is your job, during the interview, to show that you meet those expectations. Think of the process as being similar to trying out for an athletic team. When trying out for a sport, you need to prove that you have the physical skills, such as speed and coordination. When interviewing for a job, you need to prove that you have the job-related skills necessary to be successful in the position. Likewise, when trying out for an athletic team, coaches are looking to see if you will be a good "fit" as a reliable and valuable team member. An employer is trying to determine the same thing. They want to hire a dependable, productive member for their team. You can prove that you are the person they need by proving the following points: that you look like the right person, that you can be counted on, and that you can do the job.

Do you look like the right person?

- Personal appearance
- Paperwork (well-done résumé, etc.)
- Interview behavior
- Verbal skills

Can you be counted on?

- Good attendance
- Loyalty
- Dependable in completing things
- Productive

Can you do the job?

- Job-related skills
- Previous experience
- Training
- Education
- Volunteer work
- Life experiences
- Interests
- Hobbies
- Successes

Reaching Your Goal

You will get the job you want, if you:

- Commit at least twenty-five hours per week to your job search
- Arrange two interviews per day
- Do your best in interviews
- Follow up

Using the Telephone To Find and Get the Job You Want

The telephone is probably the most important tool you will use in looking for a job. Very likely, it will be the key that opens the door to interviews, so learn to use it well.

Nothing is more effective than a well-written marketing letter followed promptly by a telephone call. Bob B., for example, would have missed out on the job he wanted had it not been for a careful telephone follow-up. As a senior-level manager in a high-technology firm, Bob was feeling considerable dissatisfaction with changes taking place in his company. He decided it was time to begin a mail campaign exploring new employment opportunities.

Since the XYZ Corporation had always interested him, Bob first approached them by telephone to find out who made hiring decisions in his area. He was given the names of Mr. Applegate and Ms. Dickinson as possible contacts, and he wrote to them.

Unfortunately, Bob had been given the wrong names, which often happens; his letter should have gone to Mr. Baster. Had Bob merely sat back and waited for a response to his letters, the story would have ended there. The letters to Mr. Applegate and Ms. Dickinson probably would have been discarded or, if Bob were extremely lucky, might eventually have been transmitted to Mr. Baster, but possibly too late.

Bob was successful, however, because he made a follow-up phone call to Mr. Applegate. The executive apologized for not responding to Bob's letter and told him that he really needed to contact Mr. Baster. The XYZ executive volunteered to send a memo to his colleague, attaching Bob's letter.

Recognizing the importance of keeping control of the follow-up process, Bob indicated that he would write his own letter to Mr. Baster as well. Of course, this was followed by another telephone call to Mr. Baster. In the course of that call, Bob was able to say, "Mr. Applegate suggested that I contact you," thus lending credibility to his effort.

The letter to Mr. Baster, coupled with the phone call mentioning Mr. Applegate's name, earned Bob an interview; he was hired shortly thereafter. Had Bob not made that crucial follow-up call, gaining valuable information and getting the ball rolling, the scenario would have been quite different.

Bob's story illustrates a truth about problems inherent in mailings. In a standard letter-mailing campaign, only about 50 to 60 percent of letters get read by the proper person, despite initial phone calls. From tracking follow-ups, many studies show that some 20 percent of the letters are lost in transit, sidetracked by secretaries, or left sitting in the mailroom. Another 30 to 40 percent go to the wrong person, who may or may not take the time to reroute them. These problems can only be discovered through follow-up phone work.

Before you call:

Most people experience, at least to some degree, the terrible phenomenon of phone fright—where the mind goes blank, the palms get sweaty and the caller is suddenly at a loss for words. There are two ways to guard against this: preparation and practice.

One of the surest ways to prevent a crippling attack of phone fright is to write a script. Don't take anything for granted. Include everything, especially names, since nerves can make you stumble over the simplest things. Preparing a script also keeps you from omitting important data and allows you to carefully think about what you want to say.

Your script should include the following information: whom you are calling; who referred you; why your qualifications match the company's needs; what your specific job skills are; and why a personal meeting would be beneficial for both of you.

Go over your script. Have you omitted anything important? Do your selling points really sell? Read the script, and re-read it. It is important that you become extremely familiar with it so you can converse naturally on the phone rather than read from the script when you actually make the calls.

Practice what you are going to say. Try role-playing with a friend or spouse, asking him or her to throw you some curve balls. The more circumstances you expect, the more skill and confidence you will display in the actual follow-up process.

Finally, try recording these practice calls and listening to them. Where do you sound hesitant? Where do you pause too long? What are you saying that could be said more sharply or with more punch? The more effort you put into practicing, the better off you will be.

If, in your phone call, you succeed in establishing an appointment, be sure to confirm the name, time, exact address, and so on. Most importantly, when these things have been accomplished, get off the phone. Observe the two-minute rule; anything longer wastes your contact's valuable time.

During the call:

To make your phone call a success it is important to paint a convincing picture of yourself. You need to be brief yet thorough, demonstrating an overview of your skills, arousing the interest of the company. Give the person a reason to stay on the phone and start asking you questions.

Never ask if you have caught someone at a bad time.

During the conversation, generate interest; sell a few of your accomplishments.

Include the reason for your call and a request to meet. Make sure you close out the conversation with a question that will ensure a positive response.

After you call:

Keep records. It is amazing how many people insist on keeping the information from a follow-up campaign in their heads. Don't do it—not if you're following up dozens of letters, not if you want to maintain a careful agenda, not if you have other things on your mind (and who doesn't?). Generally, the best record-keeping system is a card file. Most people prefer filing the cards according to the date of the next intended contact; then they can simply pull out the cards for any given day to see what calls they should make.

Be thorough when you record follow-up responses, since you are unlikely to remember exact details seven to ten days later when you are calling again. Also, record your feelings concerning the response. How positive was it? Did you sense that there may be an opening soon? Do you think the person will follow through on promised contacts?

Frank C. is a classic example of someone who prepared a script, had a good filing system, and followed all the steps of proper telephone contact. A petroleum engineer, Frank suddenly found himself unemployed after twenty years in the business. Actively engaged in personal networking, he conducted a carefully orchestrated marketing letter campaign as well. Following up one letter led to a pleasant, twenty-minute visit with Bill S., field sales manager of a local oil service company.

In the course of their conversation, Bill mentioned that he knew several small oil companies in Denver that were moving from the recession into a real expansion mode. Bill promised to get a list of Denver contacts for Frank.

That night after their meeting, Frank sent Bill a handwritten note thanking him for the visit and gently reminding him about the promise of a list of names. After a couple of weeks, when his file cards showed that it was time for a follow-up, Frank placed another call to Bill's office. Since he didn't want to push too hard, he spoke with Bill's secretary, who explained that Bill had just returned from an unexpected week-long trip. This eased Frank's mind somewhat since he had not heard from Bill, but he was quite surprised to then find himself being put through to Bill.

Once on the phone, Bill actually thanked Frank for making the effort to follow up, since he had taken the time to gather the information on Denver, but his busy schedule had kept him from sending it to Frank. Bill gave him two good names and promised that more would follow.

Three months later, Frank relocated to Denver at a new career level with one of the oil companies on Bill's list. He feels sure that had he not made the second follow-up call, Bill would probably not have forwarded the names to him or would have done so too late.

Since then, Frank has maintained contact with Bill, writing him a thank-you note and meeting him for lunch when their travel schedules coincide. Frank recognizes the importance of never letting go of a good contact.

Here are some additional telephone guidelines to follow:

- Be prepared for the unexpected! You may be put through when you had planned to speak only to the secretary, or you may be screened for a particular position when you had simply been making a networking call.
- Keep your phone calls short and simple. Observe the two-minute limit. Stick to the objective of the call; avoid being interviewed over the phone.
- If you are having a problem getting past the secretary, try calling before nine, after five, or during lunch.
- Don't forget that a secretary or administrative assistant can be your biggest ally. Get that person's name and establish a friendly rapport.
- In general, avoid Monday mornings (too busy) and Friday afternoons (people are hard to reach).
- Try to make what you say sound professional and powerful. Be interesting and enthusiastic to the person with whom you are speaking.
- Learn people's names and use them. Nothing establishes rapport faster.
- Practice with low-priority companies before calling your major targets.
- Memorize your script so that you don't have to read it on the phone.

- Maintain control of the follow-up process. Say that you will call back, rather than waiting for them to contact you.

Adhering to these tips, having a good script, and maintaining careful records should make telephone follow-up calls work for you. It not only helps speed up a job search, but it is the fastest way to get immediate feedback on what you are doing.

▲ Conclusion and Activity

*Now is your opportunity to write your personal job search plan. Using the Nine-Step Job Search found in this chapter, you will define your product, identify the market, and locate possible employers. Completing the résumé worksheet found in this chapter will define your product: **you.***

Based on the information you completed, you can determine what skills and accomplishments will prepare you for your ideal job. You also can determine where your weaknesses exist and how you need to go about resolving them. If you find that you are lacking in leadership skills, for example, you can get involved in student organizations at your campus in order to gain those skills.

*Also, when researching your product (**you**), you can assess what type of work environment you want, where you would like to live, what salary you hope to earn, and what job responsibilities you hope to have. Based on this information, you can narrow down the market or industry within which you want to work. Then it is time for some in-depth research. Using some of the resources recommended in this chapter, find some companies that offer the opportunities that you are seeking. This plan will be your road map for your future job search.*

Chapter 4
Writing a Résumé and Organizing a Portfolio

INTRODUCTION

Remember when your university or college recruited you? More than likely, a representative visited your high school during an important game or event. You had one opportunity to really shine and prove that you were on top of your game. The opportunity passed quickly but paid off with large dividends in terms of scholarships, the chance to participate in athletics at the collegiate level, and the opportunity to represent your school as a student-athlete.

A résumé is very similar to that important game or event. A résumé represents your opportunity to shine and prove that you are the best candidate for the job. Employers typically spend less than five minutes reviewing a résumé, so the opportunity passes quickly. As with athletic recruiting, a good résumé will have lucrative dividends in terms of a job offer and a future career that is both satisfying and challenging.

This chapter walks you through the steps in preparing a successful resumé. This short document carries a great deal of importance and potential rewards, so it is important that you commit the time and energy it requires. Different types of resumés are described and examples are included. This chapter also discusses the use and content of portfolios.

Resumé Writing: Making a Good First Impression

Your resumé is *you*! Often the first contact with a prospective employer is made through your resumé. With this in mind, it is essential that your resumé creates a good first impression. Your resumé should not only list your accomplishments, but should also separate you from the rest of the candidates.

Your success in the difficult task of looking for a job depends a great deal on how well you are able to communicate your work experience, education, skills, credentials, and extracurricular activities. Resumés should be brief—never more than two pages—and attractive—inviting and easy to read. Any style you choose should remain consistent. Your cover letter and reference list should follow a similar style.

Which Format Should You Choose?

There are two common types of resumés: chronological and functional. A **chronological** resumé is used most frequently. It charts your work history in a reverse chronological order, listing employers, dates, and responsibilities. Chronological resumés are particularly effective if you have lots of work experience.

A **functional resumé** is created without employment dates or company names and concentrates on skills and responsibilities. It can be useful if you have changed careers or when current responsibilities do not relate specifically to the job you want. It provides first the experience most relevant to the job you are seeking, and deemphasizes jobs, employment dates, and titles.

There are advantages and disadvantages to each format. On the list that follows, check off the traits that most accurately describe your situation to determine which format would be best suited for you.

Chronological

Is Advantageous

_____ When the name of the last employer is an important consideration.

_____ When the job history shows real growth and development.

_____ In highly traditional fields (education, government).

Is Not Advantageous

_____ When work history is spotty.

_____ When you have changed employers frequently.

_____ When you are looking for your first job.

Functional

Is Advantageous

_____ When you want to emphasize capabilities.

_____ When entering the job market for the first time.

_____ When you have a variety of different, unrelated work experiences.

Is Not Advantageous

_____ When you want to emphasize a management growth pattern.

_____ When you have performed a limited number of functions in your work.

_____ When your most recent employers are highly prestigious.

A **scannable** résumé is not really another format but is any kind of résumé designed to be read by a computer. More information on the scannable résumé—and examples of chronological, functional, and scannable résumés—will be given later in the chapter.

The College Student's Résumé

Even if you have no practical work experience or a less-than-sparkling grade point average (GPA), your well-constructed résumé can still be the ticket to getting the interview. On the other hand, you can study hard in school for four years and graduate with honors. Yet when it comes time to enter the job market, the first request the interviewer makes is "to see a copy of your résumé." A good résumé, one that represents your hard-earned skills and accomplishments, will help you bridge the gap between college and the work world.

Some college grads are frustrated because they feel they don't have enough previous employment to allow them to find a decent job. They've heard so much about the importance of practical experience. Others may fear that they're good but their GPA may keep them from being considered by the companies they really want to work for. There are solutions to these and related problems.

For the majority of college students, a functional résumé that highlights skills is the ticket to getting the interview. Most college students do not have enough experience to warrant using a chronological résumé. However, a student who has had several unrelated paid jobs and has also had internships and/or volunteer, committee, or other work experience can list those unpaid though valuable assets under "Experience" in a combination (functional and chronological) résumé.

Your GPA and Your Job Future

A high grade point average is certainly an asset, but it is not a necessity for finding a good job. It's true that certain corporations require a GPA of 3.5 or higher, and many management trainee programs with major retailing chains require at least a 2.9 for recent grads or students. But the key word here is *students*. Once you've been working at a company for three years, you are no longer a recent graduate and will not be treated as such if you apply to some of the businesses that previously wouldn't look at you. With three years of job experience, you will probably not be asked for your college transcripts unless applying for a job in the field of education. You see, your GPA will not follow you around for the rest of your life.

When companies visit your campus to interview students, you can read their promotional material to see which ones have that 3.5 or higher GPA requirement. Or you can ask your school's career center for the information. If your GPA is lower, apply for a position at the many fine companies that do not have the requirement. Then, after three years of professional work experience, if you still wish to do so, interview with the corporation you originally wished to work with.

College Graduates Stepping onto the Corporate Ladder

Some college grads have previous paid experience involving skills that directly relate to the jobs they're applying for. Let's say, for example, that during your last two years of college, you had a part-time job as an engineering trainee; and now, as a graduate, you are seeking a position with larger engineering firms in another city. You would use the **chronological résumé** to detail your job experience that points you in the direction of your future position.

What if you have no paid experience? Many college students do not have any paid job experience that ties into their job objective. That might seem like an insurmountable barrier, because as we all know, many companies won't hire someone until he or she has experience in the field. But how do you obtain experience if no one will hire you?

Well, don't give up. Most students have some sort of related experience to write about in their résumé for that upcoming job or they wouldn't be interested in applying for it. Think back over your school years. Perhaps you worked on school projects related to your job objective. Or what about those committees you've been an active member of? And don't forget volunteer work in your field. Also include any special achievements that are directly related to your career objective.

Students, Grads, and the Two-page Résumé

As is true even among most professionals, students and recent grads should be able to create a one-page résumé. But some grads may have an abundance of related experience requiring a two-page résumé. That is all right. It is better to have a well-written and properly formatted two-page résumé than a poorly written, crowded one-pager. Don't use a smaller typeface in hopes of getting all the information onto one page. Such a tactic will hinder rather than improve your job chances. No employer wants to bother with a hard-to-read résumé.

Tips

- Add "More" or "Continued" at the bottom of your first page.
- Place your name and "page two" at the top of the second page.

Résumé Preparation

The résumé is a very critical element in the job search process. Its purpose is to provide a brief, attractive, easy-to-read summary of your qualifications for employment. It should not be a life history or include information that would have negative or neutral impact on your prospects for employment. It should be error-free and present credentials in a positive but honest manner.

Primary Components

The résumé will have several sections, which will include certain pertinent information.

1. **Identification.** Include name, campus address and permanent address (if necessary) with ZIP code, telephone numbers (including area code), and e-mail address.

2. **Career or Job Objective.** This section is optional and should not be included if your career goals are not concisely defined. If your objectives are very specific, however, you should make a brief statement describing exactly what you are looking for, possibly a specific job title or titles. If your goals are very broad, or you are qualified for and considering several unrelated jobs, you may want to consider more than one résumé. Use phrases rather than complete sentences, and avoid general statements such as "opportunity for advancement," "a challenging position," or "a progressive company."

3. **Education.** List schools attended, beginning with the most recent; include the name of the school, location, your graduation date, degree, and major/minor. Include relevant training and continuing education. You may also describe briefly your curriculum, abilities, skills, and competencies as they relate to the type of employment you are seeking. You could mention scholarships or the fact that you financed all or a portion of your college expenses. It is a good idea to include your grade point average. Most potential employers would notice its absence and could possibly assume the worst. Include certification (for teaching or other professions), if applicable.

4. **Work Experience.** List your previous employment (full-time, part-time, internships, or co-ops) in reverse chronological order; that is, most recent first. Include dates of employment, company name and location (city and state are enough), and your job title. Describe your responsibilities using phrases beginning with action verbs, in present or past tense, depending on the time of the experience. If you've held many jobs, you may want to be selective as to which to include on the basis of relative importance to your current goals and how recent the employment was. Some college graduates do not have sufficient paid work experience for a résumé, but through special class projects, unpaid internships, volunteer jobs, and extracurricular activities have obtained valuable and marketable job skills. These could be included with the small number of paid jobs under the heading "Experience."

5. **Professional Sports.** This experience can be listed separately or included under "Work Experience." Include the team, years played, position, awards, distinctions, pertinent skills, and knowledge acquired.

6. **Extracurricular Activities and Honors.** List your professional affiliations, clubs/organizations, campus activities, and dates of involvement. Include any offices you held or committees you chaired. Briefly describe any activities that might be unfamiliar to prospective employers. List your honors and awards here or, if you have received several, in a separate section.

7. **Further Information.** This is your opportunity to include any pertinent information that did not fall into any previous categories. Transferable skills, such as technical capabilities and foreign language fluencies, are especially important for student-athletes who lack experience. Time management and team leadership are also transferable skills, You may also choose to include miscellaneous personal information such as your willingness to travel or relocate, dates of availability, and related hobbies or special interests.

8. **References.** The optional statement "References available upon request" should suffice. Have a separate sheet listing names, titles,

---

AREAS OF EXPERIENCE

Even as a college student-athlete, you may have more "experience" to include in your résumé than you realize.

Work
- Paid/unpaid work
- "Informal" work - babysitting, family farming, or lawn-mowing
- Volunteer/job-related hobbies

School/Extracurricular
- Vocational training program
- Other related courses
- Extracurricular activities including clubs and sports

Hobbies/Family/Nonwork
- Volunteer work/church activities
- Special interest activities
- Experience that required responsibility, hard work, or special knowledge

Functional-Style Résumés

Chronological Résumé Format

NAME

School Address City, State, ZIP School Phone Number e-mail address	Permanent Address City, State, ZIP Permanent Phone Number

EDUCATION: List most recent first. State name of university attended, degree received, major field of study, option, minor, certificate awarded.

AFFILIATIONS AND AWARDS: State position of office held, organization, team dates of involvement, and describe your activities. If your work experience would make you more marketable to a potential employer, put the work experience section here and this section below.

WORK EXPERIENCE: Begin with the most recent first. List dates, job title, name of organization, address, and description of duties. Include strong action verbs to begin your descriptions and emphasize skills that are transferable to the work you are seeking.

SPECIAL SKILLS: Language fluency, knowledge of computers or other office machines (including specific types), or other special talents that are relevant.

REFERENCES: This line is strictly optional. If included, simply state "Furnished upon request." Have a separate references page prepared and ready to show to a potential employer if asked.

Sample Résumé

Name
804 Hawthorne
Somewhere, TX 77800
(409) 555-7013
e-mail hello@hotmail.com

EDUCATION
Midland College, Midland, TX
Bachelor of Science in Industrial Engineering, August 19xx to May 20xx
Major GPA: 3.57; Overall GPA: 3.03

TECHNICAL EXPERIENCE
- Gained hands-on experience with the conversion from manual to automated incentive plan system
- Worked with a variety of systems: MOST (Vax), MAPPEP (IBM), TSO (IBM), STARS (IBM), and PRIME (IBM)
- Exposure to the corporate environment, which included weekly status meetings, project presentations, and critical deadlines

WORK EXPERIENCE
Carrier Air Conditioning—Untied Technologies
Industrial Engineering Co-op Student; Spring/Summer 19xx, Fall 19xx
Major project work included:
- Developing weekly S.H.P. labor control summaries
- Implementing computerized incentive plan
- Shop tracking activity reporting
- Developing standards
- Cost development of manufactured parts
- Supervising five-person team during annual inventory

Midland College
Student worker—averaged 25 hrs/week; August 19xx to present
- Worked in several campus departments while pursuing degree
- University Honors Program—coordinated High-School Enrichment Program
- Career Center Placement Office
- Physical Plant
- Math Department—tutored students

MEMBERSHIPS
- Student Engineering Council—Co-Director for Fall 19xx CEO Career Fair
- Member of the Institute of Industrial Engineers—Midland College; Chairman of Student Advising and Résumé Book
- American Production and Inventory Control Society
- Hospital Management System Society and Peer Advising
- Men's Basketball Team at Midland College

References available upon request

Résumé Preparation 69

Functional Résumé

Rochelle Jones

123 Camp Rd
Anywhere, USA 77800
(410) 555-3333
john@anyu.edu

432 Parents Lane
Somewhere, TN 76543
(512) 555-9999

PROFILE Outgoing personality—thoroughly enjoy assisting others—highly creative —motivated—quick learner. Willing to relocate. Welcome extensive travel.

EDUCATION Big Time University, Anywhere, USA
Bachelor of Arts and Sciences May 1997, Psychology, Major GPA 3.3/4.0 Overall GPA 3.0/4.0. Achievement: Worked full-time while in college to fund expenses.

ACHIEVEMENT

LEADERSHIP
- Athletics—track and basketball.

ARTISTIC EXPRESSION
- Studied theater, acting, film and cinema and performed in several plays, skits, etc. before audiences.
- Acquired skills in script memorization, voice diction, set and prop design.

SERVICE TO OTHERS
- Actively participated in Alpha Omega Sorority and held several positions of leadership: Historian, Vice Chairman of Social Activities.
- Received the "Silver Lyre Award" for academic excellence.
- Volunteered time and resources to the County Domestic Violence Shelter. Coordinated games and activities for children living in the shelter.

INITIATIVE AND MOTIVATION
- Conducted a self-directed search for an appropriate internship to further enhance skills in psychology.
- Contacted several organizations, arranged meetings with employers, and acquired an academic sponsor without outside assistance.

SALES AND CUSTOMER SERVICE
- Suggested creative ways for restaurant servers to generate more sales by introducing various contests and incentives.
- Consistently obtained greater "per ticket" sales from each customer by recommending additional menu items or suggesting higher-priced brand names for beverages. Established strong customer rapport, which insured repeat business.

WORK HISTORY

1996 to present	WELL OIL COMPANY	Anywhere, TN
1995 to present	HAMBURGER HEAVEN	Anywhere, TN
1994 to 1995	MY FAVORITE RESTAURANT	Sarasota, FL
	In-Store Trainer/Shift Leader	
1990-1994	SIGN DESIGN	Cookville, TN
	Graphic Artist: Computer Aided Design	

Chronological Résumé

Joe Bigtime

804 Hawthorne
Anywhere, TX 77840
409-555-7013
e-mail: name@aamu.edu

1082 Country Lane
Somewhere, TX 77042
713-555-5544

EDUCATION
Big Time University, Anywhere, TX
Bachelor of Science in Industrial Engineering: August 19xx to May 19xx
Major GPA: 3.57; Overall GPA: 3.03

TECHNICAL EXPERIENCE
- Gained hands-on experience with conversion from manual to automated incentive plan system
- Worked with a variety of systems: MOST(Vax), MAPPEP(IBM), TSO(IBM), STARS(IBM), and PRIME(IBM)
- Exposed to the corporate environment through weekly status meetings, project presentations, and critical deadlines.

WORK EXPERIENCE
Big Time University
Student Worker averaged 25 hrs/week; August 19xx to present
- Worked in Several campus departments while pursuing degree
- University Honors Program—Coordinated High-School Enrichment Program
- Career Center Placement Office
- Physical Plant
- Math Department—tutored students

Industrial Engineering Co-op Student; Spring/Summer 19xx, Fall 19xx
Major project work included:
- Developed weekly S.H.P. labor control summaries
- Implemented computerized incentive plan
- Shop tracking and activity reporting
- Developed standards
- Cost development of manufactured parts
- Supervised five-person team during annual inventory

MEMBERSHIPS
- Big Time University Football Team
    - Big 10 Championship Team
- Fellowship of Christian Athletes
- Student Engineering Council—Co-director for Fall 19xx CEO Career Fair
- Institute of Industrial Engineers—BIGU Chairman of Student Advising and Résumé Book
- American Production and Inventory Control Society
- Hospital Management Systems Society and Peer Advising

References available upon request.

business addresses, and phone numbers of three to five references. This can be mailed under separate cover or brought to the interview. As a courtesy, you should seek prior approval from the individuals you wish to list and also provide them with information about the position(s) you are seeking.

Format

1. **Length.** Limit your résumé to one page unless a second page is essential for relevant details or extensive work experience.

2. **Arrangement.** Arrange categories/sections in order of relevance, presenting your most marketable information first. Select the style that is most appropriate for the amount of information you must include. The best résumés are simple, concise, and uncluttered. The use of underlining and capitals to accent headings adds to the distinctiveness of your résumé, but do not overdo it or your résumé will look cluttered. Several revisions may be necessary to arrive at a form you find both attractive and easy to read.

3. **Paper and Duplication.** An 8 1/2"-x-11" sheet of high quality white or off-white bond paper is easy to handle and a good choice. Professionally printed copies are quite acceptable. Typeset printing is expensive and generally not necessary. Copies printed on a high-quality printer from a personal computer are also acceptable. Always use black ink.

Language

1. Use brief, descriptive phrases rather than full sentences.

2. Do not use first person singular (I, me, my, mine). Be matter-of-fact; do not praise yourself. Example: use "Awarded Outstanding Student Teacher Honor," not "I received the Outstanding Student Teacher Award."

The Scannable Résumé

Creating a computer-scannable résumé can be extremely beneficial to your job search. Why? Because as technology advances, more employers are using scanning software to manage the résumés they receive. In addition, a scannable résumé is easy to post on the World Wide Web, and opportunities abound there. Getting your résumé out to the world via computer can expand its reach dramatically, connecting you to perhaps millions of perspective employers.

Preparation

- All the information on the résumé must be in a format so that it can all be read by an optical character reader, which scans the printed data and identifies the characters (optical character recognition or OCR).
- The résumé should be printed on plain paper with black ink and limited to one or two pages. Your name and contact information should appear at the top of each page.
- Avoid using any special typefaces or graphics, such as italics, underlining, columns, boxes, shading, and horizontal or vertical lines. These typefaces or graphics are hard to scan and make the résumé look awkward on the screen. Use an 11- or 12-point type in a popular, nondecorative font. Do not compress space between letters. Boldfaced words are scannable.
- Note that most companies program their computers to pick out keywords on résumés to determine which individuals to interview. Look for these keywords in job descriptions, want ads, annual reports, and professional organizations in your field, and use them.
- Mail your standard-size résumé in a large, flat envelope. Do not fold your résumé because creases make it difficult to scan.

Format

- The most effective electronic résumé format is a combination of functional and chronological.
- Use each employer's name as a section heading.
- List your position titles below the employer's name.
- Write qualifications beneath each title in three to five clear, strong statements.
- Use bullet lists to demonstrate what you've accomplished and could do again for a new employer (quantify results).
- Consider inserting a "Summary" paragraph near the top of your résumé, using important keywords that identify your skills and qualifications.

Advantages

- Electronic résumé programs are fast and more accurate than the human eye

Scannable Résumé

Name
2304 Auburn Court
Somewhere, USA 77840
Phone: (409) 555 - 3418
e-mail: name@bamu.edu

EDUCATION
Bachelor of Science in Computer Science, Graduation - May 19xx
GPA: 3.57
Bachelor of Science in Physics, Graduation - December 19xx
GPA: 3.32
Big Time University, Somewhere, USA.

PROGRAMMING LANGUAGES:
ADA, C, C++, BASIC, FORTRAN, Pascal, PL/1, LISP, IBM 360 Assembler, HTML

WORK EXPERIENCE
Career Planning and Placement Office
Student Technician; January 19xx to present
Maintain computer systems for a local area network (LAN). Operate and maintain Placement Office software. Design and update home page for use in remote transactions by students on WebWalkUp software. Design and implement programs to print and distribute Placement Office schedules and tracking of information distribution for on-campus interviewing process.

Texas Engineering Experiment Station, Big Time University
Student Worker: January 19xx to December 19xx
Maintained subscription database for chemical data publications. Prepared publications for e-mail and regular mail-out.

Geosource Inc., Programming Department, Houston, TX
Technical Systems Student Worker; May 19xx to December 19xx
Wrote geophysical applications software for microcomputers. Designed, documented, and implemented a sonic well-log calibration package and a refraction statistics package. Taught course in basic microcomputer use.

ACTIVITIES AND AFFILIATIONS
State Championship Swimming Team
Athlete Alliance
Student Athlete Advisory Committee
Engineering Student Advisory Council
Red Cross
BAMU Sailing Club
Allemanders Square Dance Team

OTHER INFORMATION
Financed 80% of College Expenses. Past two years 100%.
Interest and experience as a hobbyist in electronics.
Strong interest in languages and travel; willing to relocate.

- Choosing the right keywords ensures your résumé is far more likely to be selected for further review after a computer scan
- Scanning programs can hold résumés until it runs out of memory
- Chances of getting an interview are better if your résumé is already in the computer
- Electronic résumé databases can be accessed by every recruiter within an organization nationwide
- The Internet has 1,800 employment-related sites; scannable résumés are available to staffing professionals via the Internet
- Fifteen percent of executive search firms and 11 percent of human resource directors scan résumés into databases
- The electronic route is the quickest route to connect with hiring managers

One Final Tip

It's advisable to have two versions of your résumé: one for the human eye and one for scanning. Offer both versions to recruiters. Your thoroughness and ability to keep up with the times will impress them!

Source: Electronic Résumé Revolution, Joyce Lain Kennedy and Thomas J. Morrow.

The National Employment Weekly, "Advice on Writing Résumés That Can Be Scanned Easily," August 3, 1996.

Action Words That Create Strong Impact

Action verbs are active-voice verbs used as the opening word of each accomplishment statement to communicate your skills and how those skills generate accomplishments. Use action words to capture the employer's attention and help him or her see your strengths and accomplishments in terms of quantitative or qualitative dollars and percentages. Remember that scannable résumés in particular need strong action words that computers may be programmed to pick out.

Action verbs that address your planning skills include:

| conceived | formulated | projected |
| created | initiated | reorganized |

Action Words That Create Strong Impact

designed	innovated	revised
developed	instituted	scheduled
devised	invented	solved
engineered	justified	systematized
established	laid out	tailored
estimated	organized	transformed
experimented	originated	
formed	planned	

Action verbs that address your skills in directing others include:

administered	determined	ordered
approved	directed	presented
authorized	guided	regulated
conducted	headed	specified
controlled	led	supervised
decided	managed	trained
delegated		

Action verbs that suggest you have skills in assuming responsibility include:

accepted	described	maintained
achieved	developed	operated
adopted	discovered	overcame
arranged	doubled	performed
assembled	established	produced
assumed	evaluated	received
attended	experienced	reduced
audited	gathered	reviewed
built	halted	sold
checked	handled	transacted
classified	implemented	tripled
collected	improved	used
compiled	initiated	utilized
constructed	made	

Action verbs that show an ability to provide effective service include:

carried out	explained	provided
committed	facilitated	purchased
delivered	furnished	rewrote
demonstrated	generated	sent
earned	inspected	serviced
exchanged	installed	submitted
expanded	issued	transmitted
expedited	procured	wrote

Action verbs that suggest you have interactive skills include:

advised	coordinated	negotiated
aided	counseled	participated
apprised	helped	promoted
clarified	informed	recommended
conferred	inspired	represented
consulted	interpreted	resolved
contributed	interviewed	suggested
cooperated	mediated	unified

The following are examples of completed accomplishment statements using action verbs:

- Achieved a 25% cost reduction by creating and installing a complete accounting system by department in a large agency.
- Created a profit and 1088 statement, by product, resulting in substantial increase in sales in the high-profit products.
- Managed a professional group in creating a sales organization after identifying a $300 million market.
- Conceived a new management information services procedure that made vital operations reports available to management the following day.
- Developed a community acceptance campaign in San Francisco, resulting in the reduction of processing time by nearly 25%.
- Revised shipping procedures and introduced improvements that substantially reduced costs and shipping time.

- Discovered $190,000 overstatement of a division's inventory, enabling corrective action by management.
- Trained new employees in laboratory procedures and use of equipment, resulting in more effective and efficient job orientation.
- Reduced turnover of personnel from 17% to 9% per year.
- Installed a cost system for complex fabricating process, saving $75,000 per year.

Action words convey involvement, accomplishment, and leadership. They produce a strong impact on the reader. Try to use them, where applicable, not only in your résumé, but also in cover letters and thank-you notes.

Final Résumé Pointers

1. Accent only your positive points, not the negative. Don't mention, for example, that you were fired or are divorced.
2. Don't be too modest. This doesn't mean you brag about how "brilliant" you are, but do include information that will help you stand out above the others.
3. Don't include dates if they work against you. Employers look for stability, not six months here and two months there.
4. Do not include a salary history. You don't want to be restricted by your last salary.
5. Do not include special interests or other personal information unless it clearly adds to your ability to do the job you are seeking.
6. Make sure your résumé is attractive. It should be neatly typed and have large margins.
7. Evaluate your résumé: It should be easy to read and highlight key-words and phrases.
8. Have someone else check it for correct spelling, grammar, and punctuation.
9. Allow yourself plenty of time to prepare and review the résumé and receive feedback from others.
10. NEVER lie on your résumé. Dishonesty is at the top of most employers' list of complaints. In fact, it can wipe out every good accomplishment you have.

A résumé is . . .

- Expected from you by many employers.
- A quick way to make an impression—either good or bad.
- A way to answer "Why should we hire you?" by providing related skills, accomplishments, and experiences.
- More likely to get you screened out than in—especially when used in the traditional way.

A résumé is not . . .

- The only tool for getting interviews.
- Going to get you a job offer.

The Portfolio

A portfolio can be used for "show and tell" during an interview. Your portfolio should contain those projects that provide evidence of your skills and accomplishments. Employers will want to know what you can do and what you have done, and past evidence is one of the best ways to demonstrate yourself to them.

To begin your portfolio:

- Decide what to carry your portfolio in: binder, box, or zippered case.
- Save class papers and projects.
- Save any proposals or projects done in activities outside of class.
- Save projects from any work experience.
- Save projects that were done with video, in photographs, or on disk.
- Make a brief description of each project and what skills you demonstrated in it.

Why Should You Use a Portfolio?

An employment portfolio sets you apart from other candidates. It demonstrates your unique talents and abilities to the employer. The items in your portfolio illustrate your style, ability, and creative potential, thus supporting what you, and your résumé, tell the employer.

Items to include

- A program from an event you planned.
- Awards, honors, certificates for special training.
- Items you have created (e.g., teaching tools, art projects, special reports).
- Documentation of technical or computer skills that could benefit the employer.
- Letters of commendation or thanks from people you have worked with.
- Newspaper articles that address achievements.
- Reports of career-related work experiences (e.g., student teaching report, internship, or co-op summary).
- Sample lesson plans or other papers you may have prepared as a part of your training.
- Pictures that demonstrate special skills you have or clients you worked with.
- An official copy of your transcript and other official certifications from your discipline

Your portfolio can be organized in several ways: chronologically; with similar items grouped together; for impact, with best examples first; or in whatever order you'd like to present your work during an interview.

How to Use Your Portfolio

There are two methods to use when introducing your portfolio in an interview: the wait method and the upfront method.

The *wait* method means waiting for an interviewer to ask a question about your knowledge and skills. At that time you are able to put the portfolio into action by showing the interviewer the answers from your portfolio.

When using the wait method be sure to have done your research, finding out what competencies the employer is looking for. Then put into the portfolio those projects that the employer would find desirable.

Once you are able to introduce your portfolio, you are able to have some control over the remainder of the interview.

The *upfront* method is used when you walk into the interview and make it very obvious to the employer that you have a portfolio that you would like to share, by placing it on the table while shaking the interviewer's hand or just afterwards. Many interviewers will be curious about the presence of the portfolio and will ask you about it.

Remember, a portfolio is your opportunity to *shine* and will help you stand out from the other applicants!

▲ Conclusion

Many students feel that they are too young to start work on a résumé. On the contrary, even if you're a freshman, it's not too early to begin your résumé. If you wait until the last minute, it is more likely that your résumé will have errors or you will have forgotten important events that should be included.

Start your résumé now and build on it each semester. If you make the effort to constantly update and refine your résumé, you are guaranteed that it will be a complete and effective document by the time you are ready to show it to employers.

Many students feel that they are too young to start work on a résumé. Whether you are a freshman or a senior, the time is right for you to write a résumé. If you wait until the last minute, it is more likely that your résumé will have errors or you will have forgotten important events that should be included on your résumé.

Start your résumé now and build on it each semester. If you make the effort to constantly update and refine your résumé, you are guaranteed that it will be a complete and effective document by the time you are ready to provide it to employers.

Your résumé has one goal: to get you interviews. It has to make the strongest possible case for your candidacy, creating an image that will make people want to meet you. Employers hire people to solve problems and meet specific needs. Detailing results-oriented accomplishments and tailoring the résumé to a specific employer's needs will greatly increase your chances of landing an interview.

▲ Activity

Using the tips and examples from this chapter, write a rough draft of your résumé. The résumé worksheet that you completed in chapter 3 will be especially helpful. Give a copy of your résumé to at least five people and ask for their opinions. Share it with your coaches, your academic advisors, your family members, and a member of the career center at your campus. They can provide you valuable suggestions to improve and enhance your résumé. Once you have received their suggestions, make the appropriate changes. Most importantly, update your résumé at the end of each semester with accomplishments or activities that occurred during that semester. Your final product will be well worth the effort.

Chapter 5
Networking

INTRODUCTION

Have you heard the expression, "It's not what you know, but who you know"? When it comes to your job search, this expression usually proves correct. Many people view networking as a negative activity. After all, who wants to "use" their friends?

Networking, however, is not "using" your friends. Rather, networking is a way to share information about job openings and qualified job candidates. The more people included in your network, the greater the chance that you will hear about job openings. Likewise, the larger your network, the greater the chance that employers will hear about you when they have job openings.

Your network is already pretty large. If you do not agree with that statement, this chapter will prove to you just how large your network is. It will also provide you with tips on how to improve and expand your network.

Networking the Right Way

Many business executives define networking as "using my friends to find a new job." This definition couldn't be further from the truth. The essence of effective networking is building relationships—not using people. Networking is a powerful way of building professional relationships. It is a process of actively fostering contacts and creating ways to disseminate information. In its purest form, networking is an art that allows employed managers and job hunters to acquire the information they need to make intelligent career choices.

The speed at which you get a job or internship is directly related to how many people are in your network and how many of them know your qualifications and what you are looking for. Nearly 65 percent of all job openings are never advertised or listed with employment agencies, and more than 70 percent of all new jobs are created by small businesses. This hidden job market is difficult to access through traditional job search methods. That's why networking is so important!

Do not wait until you desperately need a network to begin developing one. Networks are based on trust, respect, and personal chemistry; they are not developed overnight. Networking is a long-term strategy. Networks improve over time as they are shaped by their members.

Making New Contacts

Write down the names of all the people you know, regardless of their connections or professions. These people could become part of your career network. After reading one operations manager's networking list, I asked why his parish priest wasn't included. The manager said he did not see why he should talk with a priest if he wasn't interested in becoming one. When I pointed out that most priests know every member of their congregation, the executive added the priest's name and called him. The conversation resulted in a referral to a business owner who needed an operations executive, which led to a job offer with a 20 percent salary increase.

There are many ways to identify networking contacts. Here are some places to find folks who may know something about a field, an organization, or a school you are considering:

- Your college alumni association or career office networking lists
- Your own extended family
- Your friends' parents and other family members

> Your professors, advisors, coaches, tutors, clergy
>
> Your former bosses and your friends' and family members' bosses
>
> Members of clubs, religious groups, teams, and other organizations to which you belong
>
> All the organizations near your home or school

Many people hesitate to contact others for the fear of imposing by asking for help. The reality: Most people are happy to do something for someone else, if asked. If however, the person you called is unable to help you, ask if he or she knows someone else more closely related to your field of interest.

Some candidates prefer to write to networking contacts instead of calling. Regardless of the method, be sure to maintain a positive attitude. Friends and business acquaintances don't want to know the details of your layoff or your worries about the future. Instead, convey that you're in control and excited about investigating career options.

Meeting with Contacts

When meeting networking contacts, don't let the conversation deteriorate into social chitchat. Instead, maintain a business focus by meeting at an office or neutral site, such as a restaurant, and take responsibility for the discussion. After some polite remarks, contacts are likely to ask you how they can help. An effective response should include your appreciation for the meeting and your purpose in contacting them. Make it clear that you don't expect a job offer, then begin asking purposeful, open-ended questions such as: How did you first become interested in your industry? Where would my skills and interests best fit in this industry or company? What are the major trends affecting the industry? How do you remain abreast of industry development? What professional organizations should I join to expand my contacts? Who else do you think I should talk to?

Eventually, you'll develop a rapport and you can ask the magic question(s): (1) Do you know of any openings for a person with my skills? If not, then . . . (2) Do you know of anyone else who might know of an opening? If not, then . . . (3) Do you know someone with lots of other contacts who might know of an opening?

Caution: *Remember that you're trying to enhance a relationship, learn from your contacts' expertise and be remembered favorably. Listen carefully and don't briskly interrogate the person.*

When you've asked sufficient questions or exhausted your allotted time, try to close the meeting in a way that leaves the door open for future contact. The following "two-part active close" can be effective:

> "Bob, this certainly has been an informative meeting. You've helped clarify a number of points about the communication industry. I'd like to keep you informed of my progress as I continue investigating the industry. Would that be all right with you? Also, since I'm actively looking for new opportunities, please keep me in mind if you hear anything."

Within a few days, send your contact a thank-you letter that reiterates your appreciation for the meeting and summarizes the points you thought were most helpful. This shows you were really listening.

Thus, the important elements of networking can be summed up in four simple steps:

1. Contact the person.
2. Follow up after your meeting.
3. Take the suggested action steps.
4. Stay in touch with the contact regularly.

The name of the game in networking is regular and consistent follow-up. If the contact welcomes the initial networking meeting and it goes well, he or she will want to hear about your progress. Remember that networking is a give-and-take process; ask your contacts about their plans and offer to help in any way you can, then back this offer with action. This process of nurturing contacts will sustain and enhance your career.

Network Mainentance Tips

The following tips will help you maintain and expand your network to help you find the position you want:

Keep accurate records. Start an address book, Rolodex, business card folder, or computerized directory with the names, phone numbers, fax numbers, and addresses of key contacts along with the dates you spoke to them and the follow-up action taken (whether it was setting up an appointment or sending a résumé). Continually update and add to your "network book." It will be invaluable. It's helpful to note next to each name such things as mutual acquaintances, mutual hobbies, or anything that will help you personalize the next contact you have with the person.

Honor your commitments, no matter how small they seem. If you agree to call someone at a certain time, do it. If the contact is unable to take your call at that time but you do get through to someone, ask that person what time would be best to call back; then leave a message that you will call again at the appointed time. Be sure to leave your phone number. This allows you the option of calling back at the best time if the contact has not called you by then. However, don't push yourself on people. If you are unable to connect after the second call, wait for a response rather than continually calling.

Make sure your calls are convenient. Your network partners may be in a meeting or working on urgent projects. Also, some people prefer to be called at the office, others at home. Be considerate of their wishes.

Take an interest in the people you meet. Ask questions that draw them out, not yes-or-no questions. The easiest way to capture their attention is to get them to talk about themselves. It's the favorite subject of most people.

Be considerate in your requests. Do not ask for sensitive information. Do not share with anyone else any sensitive or confidential information volunteered by your contact.

Try not to become too reliant on any one person. You can destroy the best of relationships by taking advantage of someone.

Always conduct yourself profesionally. Remember that the same network that helps you can also ruin you!

Effective Networking Skills

With a little practice, you may find that the networking process helps you stay upbeat and motivated during your job search. Jim Locasio, who located a sales position with a major electronics components company by networking, says, "The process keeps a candidate focused, active, and emotionally up. The feedback received through networking provided me with the strength to know that I was not alone in my career campaign—I had other people helping me."

You can create and reinforce a networking lifestyle by the qualities (such as helpfulness and enthusiasm) that you project. Making an effort to do the following will improve your networking ability and make your life more enjoyable too:

- Cultivate an open, friendly, accepting, and helpful attitude.
- Look toward adding value to the lives of everyone you meet.
- Solidify your people skills; there are helpful audiotapes, videos, and books on this subject. Listening skills, rapport-building skills, public-speaking skills, and a genuine concern for others go a long way toward building a networking lifestyle.
- Act like a host or hostess, not like a guest. Make people feel comfortable. Be a giver, not a taker. Don't wait to be introduced.
- Meet as many people as you can. There is nothing to lose by being friendly.
- Talk to people everywhere.
- Don't be afraid of rejection; it is neither fatal nor contagious. Don't take it personally, people don't know you well enough to reject you for personal reasons.
- Give for the sake of giving. Don't cultivate friends solely for your benefit.
- When doing favors for people, do them with warmth and generosity. Don't say yes when you mean no.
- Nurture your network. Keep in touch with people.
- Don't forget about your network after you have reached your goals.

Networking Do's and Don'ts

DO . . .

- join a professional organization, even if you must pay for it.
- take people to lunch—the purpose is to have a chunk of their time in which to learn from them.
- carry a set of business cards everywhere—work, the gym, social or business functions—and pass them out when appropriate.
- dress for your next job—look like you belong at the next level and get to know the people who can put you there.
- volunteer to help people in your company, above and beyond your job description; offer to help organize workshops and symposiums.
- dress well when traveling, even if you are traveling socially; you can make valuable contacts on airplanes.

DON'T . . .

- network for a job with someone you are meeting for the first time; get to know them—and let them get to know you—before you ask them for help in finding a job.

- be in it only for yourself; the principle for networking is an exchange of ideas and resources, and if you have nothing to offer, you will probably get nowhere.
- expect too much time; ask for fifteen minutes, and if you get an hour, terrific.
- call someone up and announce that you are calling to network; people will be put off if you are too obvious.
- overlook anyone; you never know who might be in a position to help you.

Surviving a Networking Event

At parties, seminars, and other group meetings you attend as an athlete, student, or organization member, you'll have opportunities to network with a number of people. Here are tips for handling those occasions.

1. Always make a nametag with your name and sport/major in clear view.
2. Start a conversation; go up to someone you don't know and introduce yourself.
3. Hand out (and collect) as many business cards as you can comfortably carry.
4. Avoid too much talk. Don't bore people with long stories about your childhood.
5. Don't wait for someone to suggest what he or she can do for you; propose how you might help your new contact.
6. Don't talk to one person too long. If a conversation gets stale, end it gracefully. If the conversation is productive, make an appointment for drinks or lunch and move on to another person.
7. Don't spend time with people you already know; instead introduce them to your new contacts.
8. Set goals for yourself; during each networking event, try to meet a certain number of people, and set a target number of follow-up appointments.
9. Keep your contacts up to date. An occasional phone call or a warm greeting at a future networking event will help to solidify your professional relationship.
10. Always begin and end conversations with a positive statement.

Remember that seminars, postgame gatherings, and other meetings are not a substitute for one-on-one meetings. They are helpful, however, in setting up one-on-one meetings with someone new.

Networking Exercise

1. List three people you interact with frequently and why.
2. List three people you do not interact with and why.
3. List three people you admire and why.
4. List three specific reasons why you personally intend to expand your network.
5. List three actions you will take to expand your network.

Requesting Letters of Recommendation

There will come a time in your job search, or even earlier in your college career, when you'll need to ask some members of your network—who know you well—for a letter of recommendation. Such letters provide employers (or selection committees) with another person's opinion of why you are right for the job, appointment, or position for which you are applying.

Who to Ask

The best people to write letters of recommendation for you are professors, coaches, employers, and advisors who have supervised and evaluated work that you are proud of. It is important that the letter writers know you well. If you keep in touch with your favorite teachers and employers over the years and share with them the development of your plans, they will enjoy having the opportunity to write letters that may assist you in progressing toward your goals. If the letter of recommendation that you are requesting is for a specific purpose, you should identify potential letter writers who have had the opportunity to observe you develop and progress in that area.

You will almost always want an academic reference written by a professor or a tutor who can communicate your skills. You may also want a letter from a person (i.e. coach) who can comment on other personal strengths, leadership skills, interpersonal skills, and work characteristics such as initiative, attention to detail, and high standards of performance.

It is most helpful if the letter writer is familiar with and can describe specific examples. All letter writers should address your potential for success in the given field.

When to Ask

As you complete a course, an extracurricular activity, or employment in which you are pleased with your achievement, you may want to request a general letter of recommendation from your professor, supervisor, or employer. If you find it difficult or awkward to request letters, remember that anyone who teaches or supervises the work of others expects to be asked to serve as a reference. The advantage of requesting a letter at the time you complete the course or job is that your performance is fresh in the mind of the letter writer, and therefore he or she can speak specifically about your accomplishments. There is also the advantage that you are in contact with the potential letter writer, whereas later on you might have difficulty finding them.

Sometime in the future, you may want to ask writers of general letters of recommendation to rewrite their letters for a specific purpose. This is not a burdensome task for the writer if you can provide them with a copy of their original letter. The major effort is the development of the first letter of recommendation about you; future editions require very little time.

How to Ask

Because you want letters that are positive and supportive, you should always give the person the opportunity to tell you if he or she feels unqualified to write for you or does not know you well enough or is too busy.

The best way to ask for a letter of recommendation is in a personal conference when you have the opportunity to discuss your reason for requesting the letter of recommendation. If you share with the letter writer your goals and aspirations, and the reasons why you are making the particular application you are asking him or her to support, it will assist that person in writing about you as you see yourself.

If it is not possible to meet with the person, the choice between making your request by telephone or by letter depends upon your relationship with the person. It is a choice based on what you feel is the best substitute for the personal conference.

What to Provide

It is important that you think through carefully what information will be helpful to the person who is writing a letter for you. It is important to refresh the letter writer's memory of the work that you have done for him or her. If some time has passed since you completed this work, you may want to supply materials such as the research paper you wrote or the special project that you did. You may also want to give a progress report on relevant experiences since that time.

For a letter of reference for a specific application, you should supply the letter writer with information about the criteria used in the selection process. This will provide the opportunity for the writer to speak about the qualities in which the selection committee is most interested.

The other kind of information you want to supply is information about yourself. A copy of your résumé, your transcript, and a draft of your application essay will assist the writer in viewing and speaking of you in a broader context.

▲ Conclusion

The approach to networkng advocated in this chapter is based on simple facts: People are the best sources of information; and the better informed you are, the better decisions you will make.

One of the advantages to being a student-athlete that was mentioned earlier in this book is that you have a golden opportunity to expand your network. Every time you travel to a competition or a game and meet your opponents and your opponents' coaches you can expand your network.

There are also other opportunities for you to expand your network simply because you are a college student. Get to know your professors. It is ironic that many of us see our professors three times a week for an entire semester, but we never take the time to truly get to know them.

▲ Activity

Make appointments with your professors so you can learn more about them. You will be amazed at how wonderfully "human" they are. Getting to know your professors will help you in your classes, as well as when you are in need of letters of recommendation and when you are searching for internships or full-time employment.

Secondly, get to know your advisors, trainers, and coaches. Each of these individuals has his or her own individual network and can assist you in some of the same ways your professors can. Also, meet your career center staff. A networking exercise that they will more than likely recommend is attending job fairs on your campus. If the idea of networking brings a sink-

ing feeling to your stomach, attending a job fair will alleviate some of those anxious feelings. Don't just simply attend the job fair, however. The objective of attending is meeting people. Introduce yourself to the employers there and learn more about them and their companies. Collect business cards and send thank-you notes to these individuals. After all, you may want to contact these employers in the future when you are conducting your job search.

In networking, as in sports, the more you practice, the better you get. Practice networking now and it will only get easier each time you do it.

Chapter 6
Researching Employers

INTRODUCTION

One of the most important tools you can have as you enter an interview is information regarding the company that is interviewing you. Many students have found that an interview will end prematurely if the employer realizes that the candidate did not conduct any preinterview research. Researching a company proves that you are truly interested in working there. It means that you are taking your job search seriously and likewise you will take a job seriously.

Conducting research will also help you in asking pertinent questions of the interviewer. You can really embarrass yourself if the employer asks you a question about his or her company during the interview and you don't have the slightest clue how to answer the question.

Many people don't research companies because they are uncomfortable with the research itself. If this is your situation, assistance is available. This chapter provides a list of resources that you can use for your research. Chapter 11, which focuses on the use of the Internet, also provides a vast number of research resources. Also, ask your career advisor or a librarian on your campus for assistance. These individuals are trained in this area and they can help make your research an easy process.

How to Research Companies and Employers

The best advice to a job seeker is to prepare for an interview by doing research on the company. This tip has received a lot of lip service, but little implementation. That's because most people find libraries difficult to use and have antiquated, stereotypical images of librarians as stern, old maids who are only expert at hushing people and collecting fines. Many otherwise capable executives become intimidated in the library. As a college student, you're probably accustomed to library research. But don't hesitate to ask a librarian for help if you get stuck. Researching companies during your job search may be the most important research you've ever done.

Good sources for company research can put you strides ahead of the competition. The following bibliography provides a variety of sources.

Information Sources/Job Seeker's Bibliography

Where to find addresses of American firms:

    Standard & Poor's: Register of Corporations, Directors, and Executives
    Standard & Poor's: 25,000 Leading U.S. Corporations
    Dun and Bradstreets Million Dollar Directory
    Dun and Bradstreets Middle Market Directory

Where to find addresses of foreign firms:

    Directory of Foreign Firms Operating in the U.S.
    Hoover's Masterlist of Major Asian Companies
    Hoover's Masterlist of Major European Companies
    Hoover's Masterlist of Major Latin American Companies

Current information about a given corporation:

    F&S Index of Corporations and Industries

Wilson's *Business Periodicals and Index*
Wilson's *Wall Street Journal Index*

<u>List of firms arranged geographically:</u>

Adams Media Corporation's Job Bank Series
Dun and Bradstreets Million Dollar Directory
Standard & Poor's: Register of Corporations, Directors, and Executives

<u>Basic information about a company's size, corporate history, etc.:</u>

Hoover's Handbook of American Business
Hoover's Handbook of Emerging Companies
Hoover's Handbook of World Business
Moody's Investor Service Moody Manuals
Standard & Poor's Corporation Records

<u>Information about an entire industry:</u>

O'Dwyer's Directory of . . . Firms series
Standard & Poor's Industry Surveys
Sports Market Place Register

<u>Information about a private company:</u>

Standard and Poor's *25,000 Leading U.S. Corporations*

<u>Information about athletics and sports:</u>

Sports Market Place Directory

<u>Information about the teaching field:</u>

The Academic Job Search Handbook
Directory of Public School Systems in the United States
The ISS Directory of Overseas Schools

<u>Information about jobs for liberal arts majors:</u>

Career Opportunities in Art
VGM Professional Careers Series' *Career in Communications*

Jobs for English Majors and Other Smart People
50 Best Companies for Liberal Arts Graduates
Career Opportunities in Advertising and Public Relations

Research about Potential Employers

Now that you know lots of sources of information, let's look at the chief areas you'll want to research about a particular organization you're considering.

The Organization's Mission

- Business field(s)
- Services or products
- Potential new markets, services, or products
- Customers or clients
- Affiliated organizations
- Its parent company, if any
- Its subsidiaries

The Size of the Organization and How It Is Structured

- Number of employees
- Its location(s) and whether it is regional, national, or multinational
- Number of plants, stores, or sales outlets
- Its divisions
- Recent structural changes
- If it is privately owned or publicly held; if it is a not-for-profit organization

How the Organization Is Doing

- If it is a leader or notable in its field
- Its financial strength/status
- Structure of assets
- Whether the organization is in a growth industry/field

- Where it invests its resources
- Percent of annual sales growth in the last five years

Industry Trends and Issues That May Affect the Organization

- Influences of government, legal or regulatory agencies
- Natural resources—shortages, excesses
- Scientific or technological changes
- International political situations
- Foreign or domestic competitors
- Social trends/lifestyles of consumers or work force

Jobs within Various Divisions of the Organization

- What people do on a daily basis
- Work responsibilities, lifestyles, work environment
- Experiential and educational backgrounds of individuals in positions within the organization.
- Typical career path

Researching the Job Market, Career Fields, and Industries

Your research should be broader than just the companies at which you plan to interview. Researching the job market is an important piece of the puzzle. How competitive are the fields you're considering? How healthy or depressed is the economy in the areas in which you are thinking of locating? Understanding the requirements and rewards of particular fields is prerequisite to deciding whether your interests and skills are a good match.

Books and periodicals, electronic resources, professional organizations, and professionals in the field are good sources of information about career fields and industries. Almost every field has one or more professional associations. Use directories such as the *National Trade and Professional Associations of the United States* to identify appropriate professional associations. You can also look in the Yellow Pages under your areas of interest and under such topics as "government," "social services," and employment." Speak with anyone who knows about a field or position that interests you. Contact companies and request annual reports, brochures, and newsletters from their personnel or public relations offices. Most companies have developed Web sites that include information on the company and its products and services.

Pick up your local newspaper or go to a library or bookstore that carries newspapers from around the country. Read feature articles, want ads, business pages, and special supplements. You can also locate some newspapers on the Internet. Also read magazines and trade journals for the formal and informal "scoop" on career fields, current issues, contacts, and openings. Read biographies or autobiographies of people who work in the field you're considering. Read recent books about the field, its history, developments, and trends.

Local Chambers of Commerce offer directories, information on business, growth, local organizations, and housing. You can Learn about many service organizations through the United Way.

State employment offices provide job listings, counseling, and training programs. Private employment agencies provide fee-paid and unpaid placements, sometimes with counseling and résumé services. Private counselors offer individualized career counseling and testing for a fee.

Finally, most college campuses, some community agencies, and even some religious organizations maintain career resource centers or provide career services.

Two Worthwhile Books

A particularly helpful resource is the *Dictionary of Occupational Titles* (DOT). It is the definitive document for cataloging jobs, profiling more than 20,000 and giving for each a standardized definition of positions and duties. It groups positions by occupational clusters and skills. The DOT is valuable as a research tool because of its comprehensive nature and concise information.

The most readily available and comprehensive resource on job prospects is the *Occupational Outlook Handbook* (OOH), a publication of the U.S. Department of Labor. The OOH is distributed every two years and is most commonly available in the reference section of college and public libraries. It profiles more than 330 occupations and millions of jobs within those occupations. The information in the OOH includes the type of work found in particular jobs, working conditions, employment statistics, training, qualifications, advancement, the earnings outlook for future employment, and sources of additional information.

The current issue of the *Occupational Outlook Handbook* offers projections on employment up to the year 2005. As you review the OOH, you may be tempted to view the data presented as the final authority on job availability. It is important to remember that, although the information presented is helpful within the context of national trends, the specifics about the job outlook in your geographic area may differ or even run contrary to those cited in the OOH.

Using Research Information for Successful Interviews

Simply being informed about an employer does not guarantee a successful interview unless you can effectively use the information. Information about the employer's products, financial data, opportunities, or how those things impact society is only helpful if you can tactfully "weave" your new knowledge into the interview. This is no easy task, and simply spouting facts or statistics—or prefacing a question with a lot of memorized information—is not the answer.

Using Information in Answering Questions

Most of the questions you will be asked in an interview will not relate directly to the information you have learned from your research. There are ways, however, to show how your skills and background meet the employer's needs, using the information you gained. Some examples:

Question: "Why do you think you might want to work for this company?"

Response: "As I understand the job, there's plenty of opportunity to be involved in both the planning of marketing strategies and the actual selling. Besides using my communications skills and knowledge of chemicals in direct selling, I believe I'm creative when it comes to marketing."

Question: "I see you're involved with the Spanish Club. What were some of the benefits from that experience?"

Response: "As secretary, I was responsible for organizing a display on Spanish literature for the Cultural Fair we sponsored. Most of my correspondence with the publishing houses was done in Spanish and I feel this experience added a whole new business angle to my fluency. I would feel very confident communicating with your international customers."

Question: "What courses did you like the best?"

Response: "I enjoyed my Sociology of Learning class the most. During one in a series of field trips, I observed a rural day-care center. That confirmed for me that this type of setting is where I want to begin my career."

Using Information in Asking Questions

Next, it will be your turn to ask questions of the interviewer. It is to your advantage to ask questions that require the interviewer to expand on information you have learned from employer's literature. Following are some excerpts from the employer literature (in bold print), paired with questions that could be formulated from the information given.

After about 12–15 months with the company, if you've demonstrated your ability, you'll be ready for promotion to Merchandising Manager. Your increased responsibility will include a larger sales volume and a number of sales associates reporting to you.

Could you talk about some methods by which trainees are evaluated?"

"What kinds of communication channels are there between trainees and the supervisors?"

"What would you say is the major quality or accomplishment that distinguishes those who are promoted from those who are not?"

Today's large store manager usually has gained experience in district or regional staff work.

"In viewing some of the background that your large store managers have, regional staff work is mentioned. Could you describe some of the responsibilities of staff work?"

From the start, ABC Company has had a goal—a vision, if you will—of being the leader in communications. That's why education, publishing, and software are among our strongest focus points.

"It appears from the brochure that education, publishing, and software are three of your key areas. Looking to the future, what are some of the current product areas that might be less important—that the company may be cutting back?"

Examples of Poor Questions

"Tell me about your training program." *(Too general—shows you didn't do your homework.)*

"At what salary level would I be if I progress to Step 3 in my second year with the company?" *(Shows your concern is money as opposed to responsibility.)*

"Could you explain your fringe benefits package?" *(Standard, boring question—needs to be more specific and ask about various aspects.)*

Asking and answering interview questions in a prepared and professional manner is the key to successful interviewing. Later, the information you gained from your research and during the interview will help you make an educated decision on whether or not to join the company if you are offered a job.

▲ Conclusion

Conducting preinterview research is very important, but a large number of students don't do it. Now that you are aware of its importance and the ease with which it can be accomplished, you should always complete research before entering an interview. Research puts you ahead of the game—and ahead of candidates who don't do it.

As was mentioned, conducting research will also assist you in making a decision about accepting a job offer. How can you make an educated decision about working for a company if you have not adequately researched it? Take advantage of the resources available on your campus to conduct the necessary research. Doing so will make you a more qualified candidate.

"Researching the company" is a critical factor in the job search. It reflects your interest and enthusiasm. During the interview it establishes a common base of knowledge, enabling the interviewer and you the applicant to evaluate the match. Candidates who have done their homework are better able to discuss how their experiences and qualifications match up with the company's needs. Candidates who are prepared can also talk about how they can make an immediate contribution to the organization. The candidate who does this is typically the candidate who gets the job offer. Researching companies and organizations is a critical step in your preparation for a job. Your future depends on it.

Chapter 7
Writing the Cover Letter

INTRODUCTION

One of the skills that employers are seeking from job candidates is the ability to communicate well. One of the best tests of your written communication skills is the cover letter that you provide with your résumé. It is a test that if failed can be disastrous. An employer will sometimes not even consider reviewing a résumé if it is accompanied by a poor cover letter. Needless to say, your cover letter is an important component of your job search.

If the cover letter is such a potential strike against you, then you may wonder why you should even submit one. Sending a résumé without a cover letter is like starting a race but not crossing the finish line or walking off the field before the final play is complete. Another example of its importance is something you probably encounter pretty frequently. How often have you read the outside cover of a novel and in less than one minute made a decision that the book was just not worth your time? On the other hand, how often have you read the outside cover and been so enticed that you couldn't wait to read more? Your cover letter will act as that enticing book cover in introducing your résumé.

The cover letter is the opportunity for you to get the employer excited about reading your résumé. After reading your cover letter, an employer will want to continue reading and gain confirmation of your skills and expertise from your résumé. This chapter will assist you in writing such a cover letter. Also included is information about job applications and how they should be completed.

Using Cover Letters

Cover letters should always be used to introduce your résumé when you cannot physically be present. Before writing a cover letter, take some time to research and understand the company to which you are sending your résumé and cover letter. You want to write a cover letter that will align your skills and experience with what the company is looking for. If you are applying for a specific job opening that you heard about through a friend or saw an ad for, carefully study the job description and match your qualifications with the desired traits. The objective of the cover letter is to impress the employer with your qualifications, motivation, and interest in the job so that he or she will want to interview you.

A successful cover letter should be written in a business format (see "General Outline for a Cover Letter") and should be both personal and specific. It should also be prepared on high quality paper, and its format should match your résumé. Each letter should be addressed to a specific person at a specific company. If you do not know who is hiring for the position/area you are interested in, call the company and ask. Don't forget to get the correct title of the person too!

The cover letter should briefly summarize your prior experience and should let the employer know what you could bring to the company. The **first paragraph** should clearly identify what job you are applying for and why you are interested in the job. If a mutual friend recommended that you apply for the job, mention his or her name.

In the **middle paragraphs**, discuss your qualifications for the job, expanding on experiences described in the résumé; make clear your knowledge and interest in the organization and in the particular job; describe specific accomplishments as documentation of the skills and work characteristics you would bring to the job. Whether this should be done in one paragraph or divided into two or three will depend on the content and what you want to emphasize. Sometimes a paragraph

General Outline for a Cover Letter

(1 inch margin minimum at top of page)

Your Street Address
City, State, Zip Code

Date

(4 returns)

Person's Name & Title
Company Name
Company Address
Company City, State Zip Code

(2 returns)

Dear Mr. or Ms. _____:

Opening paragraph: State why you are writing, name the position or type of work for which you are applying, and mention how you heard of the opening.

Middle paragraphs: Explain why you are interested in working for this employer. If you have relevant experience or education, be sure to point it out, but do not reiterate your entire résumé; refer the reader to your résumé.

Emphasize the skills, abilities, and talents you can offer the employer. Be sure to do this in a confident manner, and remember the reader will view your letter as an example of your writing skills.

Closing paragraph: Have an appropriate closing designed to facilitate an immediate and favorable reply and a suggestion that you would like further information. State your availability for an interview at the employer's convenience, not yours.

(2 returns)

Sincerely,

(4 returns)
(sign your name in black ink)

Type full name

(2 returns)

Enclosure: résumé

on relevant work experience and one on academic experience makes sense. Sometimes a paragraph on why you want this particular job and why you are qualified is most appropriate. Remember your lead sentences should state important successes and your paragraphs should be only four to eight lines long.

In the **closing paragraph**, express your interest in meeting with the employer to discuss the requirements of the job and your qualifications. Subtly imply that the employer will benefit in the long run from meeting with you.

If you have not heard from the employer within a reasonable amount of time (perhaps a week or two), telephone the individual to whom you addressed your letter to find out how the job is progressing. This will communicate your continued interest in the position and may lead to an interview.

Tips for Effective Cover Letters

- Begin your letter with a strong sentence that would make you sit up and take your feet off the desk if you were sitting in the employer's chair.
- Appeal to the self-interest of the person to whom you are writing. Include clues that indicate that hiring you will lead to higher production, greater efficiency, reduced waste, better sales, higher profit—things that will help solve the employer's problems and increase his or her own prospect for advancement.
- Include some challenging thoughts that will make employers believe that talking with you would be worthwhile even if they really hadn't been planning to hire anyone right now.
- Address any perceived deficiencies you may have by talking about strengths.
- Write in a way that reflects your individuality, but don't come across as cute, funny, or aggressive.
- Keep your letter short to hold interest (and save yourself time).

More references for cover letters:

Adams, R. (Ed.). (1995). *Adams Cover Letter Almanac*. Holbrook, MA: Adams Media Corporation.

Beatty, R. (1996). *175 High-Impact Cover Letters* (2nd ed.). New York: Wiley.

Geffner, A. (1995). *How to Write Better Business Letters* (2nd ed.). New York: Barrons.

Sample Cover Letter—No Known Opening

125 Pearl Street
Laguna Beach, CA 92651
(714) 555-3092

December 1, 20xx

Mary Smith
Section Manager
Cornwall Electronics
934 S. Bernardo Drive
San Diego, CA 92717

Dear Ms. Smith:

In May, I will be graduating from the University of California, Irvine, with a Bachelor of Science in Electrical Engineering. I am writing to explore the possibility of employment as a Control Systems Engineer at your San Diego facility.

Early in my course work at UC Irvine, I seriously considered employment with Cornwall Electronics. We use a number of your products in our laboratory work, and their design, precision, and reliability are impressive. More recently, however, I read in a professional computing journal that you are undertaking a new project to apply microcomputers in automatic control systems. Many of my electives were in the fields of control systems and computers, and I worked for three summers in microcomputer application. I believe that I am well qualified to begin my career on your new project; I know that it is directly related to my interests.

I have included my résumé, which provides additional information about my undergraduate work and campus activities. I would appreciate the opportunity to meet with you to discuss how my education and experience would be consistent with your needs. I will contact you by phone within ten days to discuss the possibility of an interview.

Sincerely,

Ray Jones

Ray Jones

Enclosure

Sample Cover Letter—Referral

543 Southwest, Apt. 103B
Allen, Texas 77700

April xx, 20xx

Edward K. Jones
Manager, Professional Recruitment
Lawry, Peterson and Zimmerman
10401 Lawrence Freeway
Chicago, Illinois 60605

Dear Mr. Jones:

I am writing at the suggestion of Dr. Wheeler to inquire about the possibility of employment with your firm as a legal research assistant. Dr. Wheeler, a professional colleague of Mr. Lawry, is my faculty advisor.

I will complete my bachelor's degree in Sociology in May from Alaska University. My work experience includes two summer internships with a large firm in New Jersey, where I had the opportunity to gain some expertise in legal research and to learn how much I enjoy it. My academic background also includes solid training and experience in research. A copy of my résumé is enclosed, which will more fully describe my qualifications.

My plans include a move to Chicago after graduation and I would welcome the opportunity to visit with you. If I do not hear from you prior to my arrival, I will call you in hopes of arranging an interview.

Thank you for your time. I look forward to hearing from you.

Sincerely,

Sean Smith

Sean Smith

Enclosure

Sample Blind Cover Letter

John Swift
105 S. College
Dickson, New York 12095

October x, 20xx

Mr. John Jones
Senior Partner
Jones, Smith, and Baker
111 West Street
Houston, Texas 77005

Dear Mr. Jones:

I am writing to express my interest in working in general management consulting. My specific interest lies in the area of long-range planning and analysis of company policies, objectives, and organizational structure and design.

A number of my previous assignments have included planning responsibilities as well as restructuring organizations to meet changing requirements. Additionally, I possess a substantial degree of experience in oral presentation, many of which were designed as decision briefings. I am currently pursuing an **MBS in Management**, which I expect to complete in December. I have enclosed my résumé for your information.

I would very much appreciate the opportunity to interview with you for any positions you might have available which match my interest and experience. I look forward to hearing from you and thank you for your consideration.

Very truly yours,

John Swift

John Swift

Enclosure

The Reality of Cover Letters

Having considered the necessity and benefits of cover letters, we must also discuss why they may be limited in value. Although we've said that the cover letter should entice the reader to look at your résumé, many employers actually go past the cover letter and straight to the résumé. They will only look at the cover letter if they are still interested after their initial résumé review. A great cover letter will not make up for a weak résumé.

Many college students end up using the cover letter/résumé mass mailing technique to convince themselves that they are actually doing something in their job search. In reality, all they are doing is generating rejection letters. Mass mailing your cover letter and résumé has extremely low odds for success in today's job market.

Understand that at the entry level, a résumé and cover letter on their own do little good. Most larger companies have established college-recruiting programs that serve as the focal point of entry-level hiring. Therefore, unsolicited entry-level résumés are often ignored and filed away. Most small and medium-sized companies do not have the internal resources to train entry-level hires, so the entry-level résumé will again be ignored. The best you can hope for in a blind mailing campaign is that you will be filed away and perhaps miraculously retrieved at some future date. This is very unlikely, however.

So when should you use a cover letter? Use a cover letter only as part of a limited, targeted campaign to reach potential employers. Remember to research the company before committing yourself on paper as its next potential employee.

Job Applications

Many employers require candidates to complete job applications prior to an interview. They will probably see your job application before they see you. Therefore, the way it is completed has a great deal to do with whether or not you get an interview. It should make a positive impression, because employers may review as many as 3,000 of them each month. The messy, illegible, or incomplete ones are discarded immediately.

A job application should be typed or filled in with a blue or black pen. Although experts disagree as to which is better, they all agree it is important to complete the form *neatly*. Therefore, try to fill them out at your own pace; don't rush.

Before you start to complete the application, thoroughly read the instructions. What a waste of time it would be for you to complete the entire application in blue ink only to find out that the company requires a typed application. Submitting an incomplete or inaccurate application can be a foolproof way to eliminate you from the running for your dream position.

While completing your application, compare it to a copy of your résumé. Many of the questions found on an application can be answered by the information you have included on your résumé. Comparing your résumé with the application will help to ensure that you do not omit any important information.

Most job application forms are similar in appearance. However, each one may ask for different information. Be aware that most employers have their own forms and will not accept copies of another application. In other words, if you apply for thirty five jobs, you will probably fill out thirty five applications.

The problem with applications is that they can reveal your weaknesses by asking, for example, about experience you do not have (something that can be avoided in a functional résumé and cover letter). Applications are designed to screen you out and are not a good tool for getting interviews. Fortunately, many small businesses do not use job applications.

Applications are important in larger organizations and government, however, and many employers request them. When you are required to fill out an application, remember these pointers:

- Follow instructions
- Be neat
- Avoid negatives
- Emphasize skills and accomplishments
- Fill in every blank
- Use an erasable blue or black pen, unless the instructions say it should be typed
- If returning the application by mail, include a cover letter

The Last Word on Applications

Job application forms have two sets of questions: (1) the printed questions and (2) the hidden questions. Employers look at your applications as a sample of your work. They look for clues about you as a worker, and their hidden questions may include:

Are you neat and careful in your work?
Can you follow instructions?

Do you make careless mistakes?

Were you prepared to complete the application?

Will you come to work prepared?

Are you honest in your answers? Can you be trusted?

How is your spelling?

Do you have enough education for the job you want?

Be sure the answers to these hidden questions represent your best work.

Remember an application *cannot* get you a job, but it may get you "screened out" of being interviewed for one! When possible, avoid the application process: *Directly contact the person who can hire you!*

When you must fill out an application, make sure that it is neat, accurate, and complete—*a positive report on you and your qualifications.*

▲ Activity

Now that you know everything you need to know about writing an effective cover letter, you need to gain some practice. Think about the ideal job that you would like to obtain upon graduation. What type of company will you be working for? What are the requirements of the position? Where will you be living? What will you be doing on the job?

Write a cover letter to accompany your résumé for this ideal job. Consider the requirements of the position and how your cover letter will prove to the employer that you meet those requirements. Make sure your cover letter is not simply a duplicate of your résumé. Instead, it should enhance your résumé and catch the employer's attention.

Have three people read and critique your cover letter. These people should be individuals who can provide valuable feedback regarding the appearance, structure, and flow of your letter. Good examples would include a career center counselor, an academic advisor, a professor, or an individual currently working in the field that you are considering. Use their feedback to improve your cover letter so that it is the best it can be.

Chapter 8
Presenting Yourself: Dress and Decorum

INTRODUCTION

Whether we like it not, others judge us by the clothes we wear. First impressions (including how we dress) are often lasting ones. In fact, an employer will sometimes make a hiring decision within the first minute of meeting a candidate. It is very important, therefore, that you dress appropriately for the interview and that you conduct yourself with the utmost etiquette.

Although you would probably rather wear jeans than a business suit, the business suit is the expected interview attire, even among companies that have moved toward a more relaxed business dress code. In other words, dress conservatively. This chapter will instruct you on the basics of business dress and etiquette.

When you interview, you can learn a lot about a company by the way that the interviewers dress. Likewise, during an office or site visit, you will gain a lot of perspective about expected attire for that company's employees. If the dress code is important in your evaluation of the company, take advantage of these opportunities to determine the company's values in this area. This may help you in making a career decision.

Dress for Success

Two questions should guide you in the pursuit of what to wear or what to buy for your career search. The first question to answer is, "What impression will I convey to others?" In business we dress to make an impression on our superiors, our peers, and our customers or clients. In a job search you want to create the impression that you are serious about searching and that you are professionally prepared to talk about your career with an executive, manager, or supervisor.

The second question to ask yourself about clothes is, "Will I look and feel confident, assertive, and self-assured?" This is a personal consideration that reflects your own tastes, judgment, and comfort level. The classic design is always in good taste. Consult with a good tailor or seamstress to ensure you know what styles fit you best. Select colors that flatter your natural face and hair coloring. But always dress in a dignified style, which will indicate that you are a confident and assured businessperson or professional.

After these considerations are taken care of, make sure your clothes are clean and pressed, fit you well, and are made of sturdy and durable yet comfortable fabrics. You can be comfortable—after all, you'll work all day in these clothes—but reflect the standards of the profession or trade and the company.

Once you have a position you want to dress in the style that seems acceptable on the job. Some technicians, once hired, wear blue jeans/shirts whereas others need to buy suits and more formal attire. Some industries require a basic uniform. The armed forces have specific uniforms for the different branches as well as for the seasons of the year. Medical jobs dictate a specific style of uniform. All businesses expect you to dress to the best of your ability when you are to meet the public that the business serves. The goal is for you to dress appropriately for the work environment while on the job.

When you wish to progress up the company ladder, find times to dress in a manner similar to your supervisors. What you wear does make a difference. Clothes send several different messages. They identify status in an organization. Clothes provide instant recognition within the company about who does what. How you are dressed can either help or hinder you in attaining your career goals.

> ### APPEARANCE COUNTS!
>
> **Clothing**
> - Conservative and neat
> - Neutrality is important
> - Conservative suit, navy blue, black, gray
> - White or pale colored shirts/blouses
> - Black or dark shoes
> - Combine personal style with good taste
> - Wear something that is comfortable and makes you feel terrific
>
> **Accessories**
> - Simple and tasteful jewelry, watches, ties, scarves, hair accessories
>
> **Grooming**
> - Hair and makeup should be neat and not attract attention
> - Scents, perfume, aftershave should be subdued—don't overdo it
> - Men, cleanshaven or beards/mustaches trimmed
> - Hands groomed and nails manicured
> - Watch what you eat before/during an interview

Whether on the job or during your job search, the most important thing to wear is your **smile**. A pleasant, open expression is one of your best assets. It's a mistake to try to appear too serious and reserved. It will seem like a false front, and in an interview you want to be yourself. When you smile, you look more relaxed and confident. And, the great thing is that smiling really does make you feel more confident. So smile, stand tall, and carry yourself with pride and conviction.

Business Etiquette

Introductions

Candidates and workers need to be aware of their personal relationships—how they deal with other people. Following correct protocol is important not only in getting the job, but in succeeding once in the workplace. Although many people are awkward and inept at introductions, there are certain dos and don'ts to follow.

The person with the most authority or the most important person is introduced first to all the others. With clients, senior executives, distinguished guests, high-ranking dignitaries, or other people of similar importance, you always introduce others to them, not the other way around.

Example: *"Senator Raven, I would like you to meet John Ascot [your own colleague]."*

In general, when introducing two people of different ages, relationships, status, introduce the younger to the older, a friend to a relative, a colleague to your boss.

Note: Even though you may be on a first name basis with your own boss, never use that first name when "outsiders" are present.

It is always your responsibility to pronounce someone's name correctly no matter how foreign that name may be to your ear. Study it and learn how to pronounce the name correctly. If you have a difficult name that others cannot pronounce with ease give them some little clue to assist their memory ("sounds like . . ."). If someone mispronounces your name, correct them gently and, if possible humorously, but do not allow them to continue to mispronounce your name.

Forgetting Someone's Name

Forgetting someone's name happens to everyone at one time or another. Simply own up to the truth by saying, for example, "I remember you very well from the seminar we attended together, but I'm having trouble remembering your name." Do not give hints about a person's name, such as, "I know it begins with a 'W.'" This is rude. You are not playing a game.

Groups and Their Introductions

When making introductions to a group either use "Ladies and Gentlemen, I would like you to meet . . . ," or, even more appropriate, introduce the client or guest to each person in the group individually. Introductions are not necessary, however, if you are with a group at a table, for example, and someone unknown to the others comes over to greet you. If you wish a moment's conversation with that person, excuse yourself to the others, and move away from the table for a moment of privacy.

Titles

Professional titles are used when you are introducing people of equal standing or rank. Official titles such as Governor, Ambassador, and Senator are retained even if the person is no longer in office. Retired military personnel retain their ranking. Individuals who consistently use first names of others but expect to be called by their titles are condescending and rude.

When introducing yourself always use your first name with your surname. Restaurants want your full name when you ask for a reserved table. The same holds true for messages you expect to be receiving.

Handshake

A handshake is a part of American business. Avoid the "dead fish" handshake. Do not put a wrestler's grip on the other person either. Extending your fingers as though you're afraid you'll catch something from the other person is equally inappropriate. Avoid also the up-and-down pump style.

Your handshake should be genuine and firm, lasting but a few seconds. Look into the other person's eyes and repeat his or her name in an appropriate greeting while shaking the person's hand. This rule applies equally to men and women in the business world. When someone offers you a hand in friendship or to seal a business deal, respond accordingly.

Your Speech

Your speech patterns reveal your education, a regional accent, your grammatical awareness, and your style. Words like *good*, *nice*, and *interesting* are bland and nondescript. The same impression may be transferred to the person who uses this "dead" language.

Strengthen your vocabulary so that you say exactly what you mean. The English language is very rich, and extending your vocabulary is a personal responsibility. You should have mastered not only the language specific to the discipline in which you work, but also the general language usage of any educated person. Avoid jargon (language specific to a given field) and euphemisms at all times. Occasionally there are words that become stylish to use. Avoid these, too. These include *hopefully*, *couch potato*, and *Freebie*, among others. Never use slang or racial slurs in your speech or writing. Likewise, avoid words that may not be known to your colleagues who do not share your areas of specialization, expertise, or education. Mispronunciation is unforgivable in a professional person. Look up the word in the dictionary if you are not sure how to pronounce it.

Improving your speech also includes listening to the tenor of your voice, learning to speak with a smile in your voice, and knowing how your voice sounds to others. Often when people hear a tape recording of their own voice, their response is, "That doesn't sound like me." This is because the speaker hears sound through head bone conduction and the listener hears sound over the air waves. Listen to yourself and adjust your speech accordingly.

Expressing Gratitude

The practice of expressing heartfelt appreciation for what another person does to help you in your work, your search for a job, or your evaluation of yourself is the standard in trade of a professional person. Thank-you notes need to be sent within twenty-four hours of the event or situation.

Such notes are appropriate any time another person has given you advice, information, suggestions, ideas, or anything else that has improved your chances of doing whatever you have set out to do in your chosen career. (See Chapter 9 for more on follow-up thank-you letters.)

▲ Conclusion

Building a wardrobe, unfortunately, takes a lot of time and a lot of money. Starting to build your career wardrobe now will help alleviate both of these problems. It is important to have the appropriate clothing by the time you are preparing for job interviews. Also, make sure that the clothing is comfortable. There's nothing worse than wearing a new pair of shoes for the first time and being in horrible pain after having walked less than five minutes to the interview site. This type of stressful situation is one that you can definitely do without. After all, you have enough on your mind during your job interview.

▲ Activity

Good advice for students who are making their first interview clothing purchases is to seek advice from professionals. We are all experts in some area, so seek out those individuals who have made it their career to assist others in purchasing appropriate business attire. Visit a local suit or dress store and spend some time with the store's staff. Let them know what type of job you are applying for so they can assist you in your clothing search. They have kept up with the most recent trends and they know what is "in" and what is "out." Take advantage of their expertise to ensure that you are truly dressed for success.

Chapter 9
Interviewing and Following Up

INTRODUCTION

It's time for the interview. This is the event that all your preparation and hard work have earned you. This is the time to strut your stuff and prove to the employer that you are the perfect candidate for their company. In athletic terms, the interview can be compared to the actual competition. You trained and practiced for weeks, even years, and now it is time for you to perform.

Interviews come in all different formats. For example, there are behavioral interviews, stress interviews, and screening interviews. This chapter will provide you with preparation skills for each of these types. Interviewing is an unnerving situation for practically everyone, so don't be worried if you are a little apprehensive about it. The best way to reduce your anxiety is to be prepared. The goal of this chapter is to provide you with the tips and resources to prepare you for this important event.

The Seven Phases of an Interview

No two interviews are exactly the same, just as no two people are exactly the same. For the most part, however, the interview process will include seven phases, many of which are within your control. For example, you should always get the process off to a good start by completing preinterview research during phase one. Phase five involves your sending a thank-you letter to the employer for his or her time in interviewing you. Completing this task could be the difference between getting and not getting a second interview.

The following phases of the interview process are discussed in this chapter (unless indicated otherwise):

1. Before the interview
   - Handle preinterview preparation
   - Research the organization (Chapter 6)
   - Arrive early and wait for the interview
2. Opening moves
   - Make a good first impression
   - Establish the relationship
3. The interview itself
   - Do your best to meet the employer's expectations
   - Handle problem questions
   - Ask questions about the job
   - Prove it!
4. Closing the interview
   - Review your strengths
   - The call-back close
5. Following up
   - Send a thank-you note
   - Get a second interview or a site visit
6. Negotiating (Chapter 12)
   - Timing of salary discussion
   - Never say "no"
   - Bracketing a salary range
   - Other fringe benefits
7. Making a final decision (Chapter 12)

Preinterview Personal Reflection Questions

Before a big game or competition, do you prepare *mentally* as well as physically? More than likely, your answer is a resounding "yes." You probably go through the same mental preparations today that you did years ago when you first started your sport. A consistent process of mentally preparing for special events is important. You need to be in the right frame of mind before the clock starts ticking or the starting gun explodes.

The same is true for a job interview. A job interview is an important event in your life. Potential employers are looking for candidates who have a firm, mature grasp of who they are, what their abilities are, and the specific types of opportunities for which they are looking. This section includes a list of reflection questions to ask yourself before you enter an interview. Answering these will prepare you for many of the questions that you will hear from employers during an interview and will give you a clear advantage during the interview competition. You will have formed concrete examples that you can share with the interviewer and you will be more relaxed knowing that you have completed your preinterview "homework."

Answer the following questions to help you describe your work attitude and characteristics:

Do you set high standards for yourself and persevere to achieve your goals? Any evidence of high achievement, such as academic honors, varsity athletics, or awards in music or the arts, is a sign that you set high standards and have the discipline to endure long periods of training and practice for deferred gratification. If you are goal-oriented, you will speak in terms of achievements rather than in terms of effort expended or functions performed.

Are you sensitive to others' feelings and cheerful and thoughtful in your interaction with colleagues? Almost all work requires that you relate to other people. Employers look for people they enjoy. They look for applicants who will be compatible with colleagues and clients.

Do you have a high level of energy and are you able to channel it into productive effort? People engaged in a variety of activities and who manage to meet their responsibilities and deadlines are people with high energy levels and self-discipline.

Are you cooperative? Do you take instruction well and work well with others? Experience in working with others on projects and programs or in team sports teaches you to be an effective team member.

Do you have the ability to lead, to organize, and to supervise other people? Leadership roles in any kind of sport or organization provide you with the opportunity to develop sought-after leadership skills. Be sure your résumé describes the leadership experiences you have.

Do you take initiative? Do you wait to be instructed before you act or do you act on your own, thinking through new ways to get the job done?

Have you had the experience of losing as well as winning? Are you able to lose and continue to give your best effort? Experience in winning and losing comes most dramatically in athletics, but there are other competitive activities in which you may have won or lost.

Are you curious? Do you seek new adventures? Are you excited about learning new skills and knowledge? Are you excited about assuming new responsibilities and learning to become more productive? Starting a new job in a new environment with new people is a risky adventure. If you have had a variety of work or travel experiences, you have learned to adjust to new situations and unfamiliar circumstances.

Do you have the capacity to be loyal? Have you committed yourself to people and organizations? Are you loyal to your friends, to your college, to former employers, to your family, to your hometown? It is not what you have been loyal to, but whether you have the capacity to be loyal that will interest employers. If you are negative and critical about your past jobs and associations, employers may fear you might be that way about their organization.

Do you have high expectations of yourself? Do you have high aspirations? Employers ask what you hope to be doing in five or ten years to get an indication of how ambitious you are.

The qualities reflected in these questions, in varying degrees, may be important to an employer as he or she evaluates candidates for a particular position within an organization. You have probably developed some attributes more than others. In your job search you should be prepared to communicate to employers through your written materials and your interview the work qualities and competencies that you have developed.

Preparation is the most important first step to interviewing. A well-prepared presentation supported by facts and examples can create a very favorable impression. Identify and focus on your skills and abilities with *specific* examples that illustrate what you say. For example, some student-athletes might say in an interview:

> "A lot of the things I learned in sports would be helpful in the business world. I developed leadership, self-discipline, and teamwork skills."

> "That's fine. But what is unique about your experiences that would make the interviewer distinguish you from the other applicants? Specific examples of accomplishments make the greatest impact:

> "A lot of things I learned in sports would be helpful in the business world. I developed leadership, self-discipline, and teamwork skills. I carried eighteen credits in a double major during the spring semester, practiced and played twenty hours a week, and served as a mentor for a twelve-year-old at a local school. I had to manage my time so that I could maintain my athletic performance, keep at least a 3.5 GPA, and continue community service, which is very important to me."

First Impressions

The first five minutes of an interview frequently lead to a decision as to whether or not you are a serious candidate. Social poise and an enthusiastic attitude will go a long way in making a positive first impression. What you communicate nonverbally as well as verbally will be important.

Nonverbal Communication

Those first five minutes usually contain many kinds of nonverbal communication—that is, sending messages or meanings to someone without words. How you dress, shake hands, walk, and sit are examples of nonverbal communication.

Be aware that the interview begins the moment you arrive at the interview site. Give everyone a friendly smile. If you come in from the cold, remove your overcoat, hat, and gloves before getting to the interviewer's office. Posture can indicate interest in the job. Walk and stand erect, but not unnaturally so. The way your body moves can communicate that you are interested, bored, or anxious. Present the interviewer with a positive image.

As you are waiting to meet the interviewer, avoid signs of nervousness such as gum chewing, finger tapping, twisting a handkerchief, or smoking. (Never smoke on the way to an interview. An interviewer may be put off by the lingering smell of smoke.) Use waiting time to your advantage. Review your skills, job application, or materials about the company.

When meeting the interviewer for the first time, have your right hand free and initiate a handshake. Your handshake should be positive—not too limp or too firm. When shaking hands, look into the interviewer's eyes and give a real, honest smile. Eye contact, your handshake, a smile, and a warm greeting set the tone for the entire interview.

After you have shaken hands, wait for the cue from the interviewer as to what to do next. He or she may say, "Let's go into my office," or simply extend a hand for you to go in. Wait until you have been offered a chair before sitting. Don't plop down or slump carelessly in the chair. This may indicate that you would be a careless worker. Even though you will be nervous, don't let your body give you away. Sit naturally in the chair and lean forward slightly—showing interest in what is being said and enthusiasm for the job.

It is important to have good eye contact during the interview. Don't let your eyes wander around the room. If there is more than one interviewer, establish eye contact with the person addressing you. Looking at the floor or ceiling says that you lack confidence in yourself or are not interested in the job. Body language can say a great deal, so know the message your body is giving the interviewer. Stay alert, be sincere, and communicate interest.

Verbal Communication

Verbal communication is sending messages to someone using words. It is just as important to *sound* like a worker as it is to look like one. The loudness of your voice, its inflection, and the words used are very important in the job interview. This is particularly true during the first five minutes.

When shaking hands with the interviewer, give a warm, friendly greeting. Do not hide your mouth with your hand, use slang, or interrupt the interviewer. "I've looked forward to meeting you," or "How are you today?" is appropriate. "How are you?" from the interviewer should be answered with a conventional, "Fine, thank you."

Use the interviewer's name in casual conversation once or twice at the beginning or closing of the interview. It shows that you care enough to know his or her name. Try to get the name of the interviewer before the interview. If not, make sure you listen carefully to his or her name during introductions. Do not, however, use the interviewer's first name unless invited to do so.

Good verbal communication means speaking clearly. Avoid mumbling or talking too softly. Let your tone of voice show enthusiasm for the job. Verbal communication also involves being a good listener. Show the interviewer that you understand the question. This could be done with a nod or a facial expression. If you don't understand the meaning of a particular word or phrase, ask. You must understand the question before you can answer it. Being a good listener shows interest in the job.

Communicate verbally what you can do for the company. Refer to your skills and interests and how you can use these to fill the job. When asked a question, be clear, concise, and to the point. Don't wander to something else without answering the question. Don't ramble on and on. And watch out for words like *stuff* and *you know*. The interviewer is interested not only in what you say, but how you say it.

Establishing the Relationship

The interview is a two-way conversation. The employer needs to find out about your qualifications for the position, and you need to determine what opportunities the organization has to offer.

The sharing of information usually begins within the first five minutes of the interview. Therefore, it is important to focus primarily on your skills as early in the interview as possible. This means knowing them so well that you can respond without having to stop and think about what to say and how to say it. Very often an interviewer's first question may be "Tell me something about yourself." In this case, you may have a chance to get across some very important items that employers look for, namely your skills, honesty, dependability, ability to get along with others, knowledge of the job, and interest in the job.

The Interview

Interviewers usually have a pattern to their line of questions. For example, the interviewer may ask if you have any leadership skills. The next question may be about school or community activities. This second question may also reveal your leadership skills and experience. Careful listening will allow you to bring these skills to the interviewer's attention.

The interviewer may ask some of the following numbered questions in order to also form an opinion about the unspoken questions (in bold):

Is the person prepared? Organized and concise?

1. Tell me about yourself. (Be concise and enthusiastic)
2. Did you bring your résumé? Transcript? References?
3. What do you know about our organization?
4. According to your definition of success, how successful have you been so far?

Is this person mature and self-aware?

5. In your current or last position, what were your most significant accomplishments? In your career so far?
6. Had you thought of leaving your present position before? If yes, what do you think held you there?
7. Would you describe a few situations in which your work was criticized?
8. If I spoke with your previous employer, what would he or she say are your greatest strengths and weaknesses?
9. How would you describe your personality?
10. What are your strong points? (Mention three or four and have one in résumé.)
11. What are your weak points?
12. How did you do in school?

Is the person motivated? What are his or her values, attitudes? Is there a fit?

13. In your current or last position, what features did you like the most? What did you like the least?
14. What do you look for in a job?
15. How long would it take you to make a meaningful contribution to us?
16. How long would you stay with us?
17. If you have never supervised anyone, how do you feel about assuming those responsibilities?
18. Why do you want to become a supervisor?
19. What do you see as the most difficult task in being a supervisor?
20. Why are you leaving your present job?
21. Describe what would be your ideal working environment.
22. How would you evaluate your present firm?
23. Do you prefer working with numbers or working with words?
24. How would your co-workers describe you?
25. What do you think of your boss?
26. Why do you want to work in a company of this size? Of this type?

27. If you had your choice of jobs and companies, where would you go?
28. If you were to design the perfect first job for yourself, what would it be?
29. What was the last book you read? Movie you saw?
30. What are you doing to reach your career objectives?
31. What kind of hours do you expect to work?

Does the person match the job and criteria?

32. What would you do for us?
33. What has your experience been in supervising people?
34. Are you a good supervisor? Give an example. Why do you feel you have management potential?
35. How have you helped to increase sales or profits? Reduce costs?
36. How big a budget were you responsible for?
37. Describe some situations in which you've worked under pressure or met deadlines.
38. In your previous position, what problems have you identified that had previously been overlooked?
39. Give an example of how you have been creative.
40. Give examples of times when you were a leader.
41. What are your goals in your career?
42. What position do you expect to hold in two years? In ten?
43. What are your objectives?

How does the person handle stress? What is their confidence level?

44. Why should we hire you?
45. You may be overqualified or too experienced for the position we have to offer.
46. Why haven't you found a position before now?
47. Do you have any objections to taking a psychological test?
48. If you could start again, what would you do differently?
49. How would you structure this job?
50. How much do you expect to earn, if we offer this position to you?

What is this person's market value?

51. What kind of salary are you worth? (Be diplomatic and cautious with reply.)

52. What other type of companies are you considering?

53. How have you kept up in your field?

Frequently Asked Questions

The following questions come up in many interviews. The comments provided after each question will help you know how to answer to your best advantage.

1. *Tell me about yourself.*

Expand on your résumé application. Explain job-related skills and interests, dependability, and honesty. You will seldom have a better opportunity to sell yourself.

2. *What are some of your weaknesses and strengths?*

Smile when asked this question. Have a list ready of what you do best. List weaknesses as possible strengths; for example, "I'm a perfectionist. But I care about the work I do and want to make sure it is done right."

3. *Why should I hire you?*

Explain all the qualities you have that would make you an asset to the company. Examples: good attendance, ability to get along with others, quick learner, skills for the job.

4. *How would you describe yourself?*

Give positive responses, for example, friendly, honest, responsible, cooperative, hard working.

5. *How do you spend your spare time? What are your hobbies?*

Relate hobbies or pastimes to the job. Emphasize skills.

6. *Why do you want to work here?*

State your interest in the company; be positive and emphasize how your skills match the job opening.

7. *Have you ever done this type of work before?*

Never answer "No." Mention similar types of tasks from past paid and unpaid experience. Also mention training/education and ability to learn quickly.

8. *Tell me about your work experience.*

Relate all paid and unpaid experience to the job opening. Again, emphasize your skills.

9. *What would you do if . . . ?*

This type of question tests your knowledge of the job. Begin your response with "One of the things I might consider would be . . . " This doesn't commit you to a perfect solution. The quality of the solution is not nearly as important as the attitude you have. A calm approach is best.

10. *Can you work under pressure and deadlines?*

This question usually means that pressure and deadlines are part of the job. Refer to skills that can help you deal with this.

11. *What are some things that are important to you in your job?*

Relate your work values to the job opening.

12. *What position are you most interested in?*

Don't give a job title. State the skills and interests you possess. Give the employer a chance to put you where you best fit.

13. *Can you get recommendations?*

This is a chance to present copies of letters of recommendation. Briefly state who wrote them and hand them to the employer.

14. *What makes you think you can do well in this job?*

Relate your interests, skills, and experience to the job opening.

15. *What kind of work are you looking for?*

State the type of job you are applying for or a position that best matches your skills, aptitudes, and interests.

16. *What do you hope to be doing in five years?*

Be prepared for this question. Have some career goals in mind. Don't respond by mentioning the salary you hope to be making or personal possessions you hope to have acquired.

17. *What have you been doing since you left your last job?*

Never say "Nothing" or that you took a vacation. If you have been unemployed for some time since your last job, be honest. State, however, that you have been looking for just the right job. Mention what you have learned.

18. *How did you get along with your former boss?*

Always be positive. If you didn't get along well, say something like,

"We sometimes had our differences, but worked together to get the job done."

19. *How do you feel about working overtime or on weekends?*

Never give a negative answer. Show your willingness to work. If your religious beliefs conflict with the question, be honest and tell the interviewer in a polite manner.

20. *What can I do for you?*

Emphasize your skills and explain what *you* can do for the employer.

Scoring Points on Tough Questions

More than likely you will be asked some tough questions during an interview. In today's highly competitive job market, probing questions have become part of almost every job interviewer's repertoire. In fact, if you aren't asked several "stress questions," it may be an indication that the interview isn't going as well as it should.

Why do interviewers use these difficult and often unsettling questions? They are used primarily to gauge how focused and thoughtful you can remain under pressure, how fast you can think, and how convincing you are. The best approach to a tough question is to examine it for what the interviewer is truly asking, answer it sufficiently, and relate your skills and abilities as best as possible.

If you practice your answers to the following hard-to-answer questions ahead of time, you will be able to field them with confidence. A little boning up before the interview can put you ahead of the many jobseekers who try to wing it.

1. Could you tell me a little about yourself?

Although this open-ended question appears innocuous, it is intimidating to most people. They don't know what to say or how long they should talk, especially since the interview is just beginning.

You should realize that most interviewers use this question not only for information gathering, but also for assessing your poise, style of delivery, and communication ability.

Instead of launching into a mini-speech about your childhood days, schooling, hobbies, early career, and personal like and dislikes, it is best to cite your more recent personal and professional work experiences that relate to the position you're seeking and that support the information and credentials on your résumé. As Kathryn and Ross Petras, authors of the book, *The Only Job Hunting Guide You'll Ever Need*, emphasize: "Everything you say about yourself should fit together to form a cohesive pattern that conveys the message: *'I have unique qualities that make me the right person to fill this position.'*"

Although this question gives you a great opportunity to sell yourself, at this stage in the interview it is better to be concise and low-key.

2. Why did you leave your last employer? or, Why are you leaving your present job?

This question doesn't require a long-winded answer, but remember to be positive, not defensive, especially if you left because of problems with your boss or co-workers. Career experts all agree on this point: Don't air your frustrations about your previous or current job or the people involved. Interviewers may interpret this to mean that you're a chronic malcontent or that others find you difficult to work with.

It is not advisable to fudge on information about why you left your last job for it can be easily checked. And if you're less than honest, the rest of your answers might be regarded with justifiable suspicion.

Perhaps the best answer to this question is simply to state that you're seeking greater opportunity, greater challenges, or more responsibility. It's not always a good idea to use "more money" as a reason. More often than not it is obvious you want a better salary when changing jobs.

3. What are your greatest strengths?

This question is a signal for you to describe your strongest attributes and skills, but be sure that you mention the specific assets that are directly related to the responsibilities of the job you're seeking. Briefly summarize your work experience and your strongest qualities and achievements. Wayne E. Calhoun, president of Professional Placement, recommends that you "be a bit pensive before answering." You don't want to sound as if you are spewing out a rehearsed list.

In today's tight job market, the four basic skills to highlight, according to Mitchell Berger, a director of an executive recruiting firm in New York, are *self-motivation, initiative, ability to work with a team,* and *willingness to work extra hours to finish the job.* You could also add such qualities as good communication skills, loyalty, reliability, integrity, promptness, and self-confidence. But try to make these abstract qualities concrete by illustrating them with incidents from your last job. Interviewers, like all other people, remember examples, so be specific. Don't say that your greatest strength is "attention to goals," that you are "motivated by challenges," and are a "perfectionist"—unless you have memorable examples to prove it.

4. What are your weaknesses?

   This question is potentially more harmful than helpful and for many people it is also one of the most intimidating. Most interviewers do not expect you to be a paragon of perfection, nor do they expect you to reveal your true weaknesses. They are just probing for soft spots.

   If you do admit a major weakness, you may win points for your honesty and openness, but your chances of getting hired are slim. On the other hand, if you give a flip answer or respond with, "Well, I don't really have any weaknesses . . . " you may annoy the interviewer with your lack of candor, arrogance, or limited self-knowledge.

   Most career advisors recommend that you turn this question around and present a personal weakness as a professional strength. As Kathryn and Ross Petras point out, "Your objective isn't to discuss your weaknesses as much as it is to discuss how and why even your shortcomings make you an ideal candidate." Let's say, for example, that your weaknesses are that you like to pay close attention to even minor details, that you are a workaholic and unable to relax, and that you neglect your friends and family when working on an important project. You can turn these weaknesses around by saying, for example, that you are very meticulous or tenaciously thorough, even if it means working after hours and on weekends to finish the job on time. This way you've cast your weaknesses as positives that most bosses would not find irresponsible.

5. What type of salary did you have in mind?

   Interviewers usually ask this question to ascertain whether the company can afford you.

   If it can be done, it is usually best to defer your answer to the end of the interview, after the interviewer has decided that he or she wants to seriously consider you. If you state your salary requirements in the beginning of the interview, your range might be either too high or too low, and this might disqualify you from further consideration. If the interviewer still insists that you name a figure, you could ask what salary range the company has been considering. If there is no answer, or no satisfactory answer, and it is impossible for you to stall any further, name a figure that meets your requirement and the standards within the industry. It is better to err a little on the high side since the final offer is invariably going to be a lower figure than you requested. It is, however, advisable to emphasize that it's the nature of the job and not the actual salary that is of primary interest to you. You can, however, include benefits paid by your current employer, such as health insurance, in your current salary.

If the interviewer asks what salary you are making now, or were previously making, you have no choice but to be honest because the figure can be easily verified.

6. What do you like most/least about your present job?

Concentrate on areas that are in some way relevant to the position you're applying for and be specific in your response. If the items you choose to discuss are couched in vague or general terms, it will reflect negatively on what type of a performer you'll be. Your answers will also provide the interviewer with clues about the type of environment or corporate culture you're seeking.

When discussing least-liked aspects of your present or previous job, try to cover some area of responsibility that is far removed from any of the functions of the job you're seeking. But be sure to frame your answer so that it shows you did a good job or you learned something new that you might be able to use in the future. This way you turn a negative into a positive and show that you are able to stick with tasks that do not particularly interest you.

7. Are you applying for any other jobs?

In today's job market hardly anyone expects you to say "no" to this question. If you do, the interviewer may think you're either naive about business conditions or not very serious about looking for a job. In your answer show that you are in the process of exploring several openings to find a good fit with your talents and potential.

It would be a mistake, however, to state that you are already weighing several offers. Interviewers are drawn to job candidates who really want to work for the company. Candidates who say, "I think I'm interested . . ." usually lose to those who know they are interested and are enthusiastic. On the other hand, don't let your enthusiasm inadvertently convey the message that you are desperate for the job and have been turned down by other employers.

8. Why should we hire you?

Although this blockbuster question presents job candidates with perhaps the best opportunity to sell themselves and impress a prospective employer, few realize what this question covers and hence utilize it ineffectively. As Marian Faus, author of *The Executive Interview* points out, the interviewer who asks you this is really probing for four qualities: your readiness for the job, your ability to handle it, your willingness to work hard at it, and your fitness for the job.

You demonstrate your readiness by describing how your work experience, career progression, and strongest qualities and achievements can make you an asset for the company. Your ability can be highlighted by discussing your specific skills and accomplishments. Your willingness can be demonstrated by your assertiveness and your attitude of commitment to whatever challenges you undertake. As for your fitness for the job, add to all of the above that you are reliable, have integrity, and can flexibly accommodate yourself to any difficulties the job entails.

Some candidates, when responding to this question, make the big mistake of going into great detail of what they hope to gain from the job. To rephrase John F. Kennedy's famous statement, "Ask not what the company can do you for you, ask what you can do for the company." As Robert Hecht, a career consultant, points out, "In return for the money and compensation package an employer offers, the company will be expecting a return on its investment. Will the company make more money, save money, or do something better and faster if you are hired? That's really what getting the job is all about."

9. Where do you hope to be in five years?

Your answer to this question should convey a commitment to the company hiring you. The worst answer you could give to this question is to state that you want to be president of the company or that you expect to occupy the interviewer's position. This sounds either too flip or too threatening. Marian Faus suggests that you talk about what motivates you, especially what will motivate you about this job. She also adds this advice: "Without saying you want the boss's job, describe where you would like to be in your career in five years, as well as what you hope to have accomplished."

Employers generally prefer people who think in terms of the future and who are capable of setting realistic goals. Saying that you're not sure, or that you have no clear-cut idea of where you would want to be in five years, may undermine your chances of landing the job. "Answers like this are a turnoff," says Annette Robson, professional employment manager at UNISYS in Philadelphia. "I'm looking for people who know what they want to do and who believe that their goals and the company's are in sync."

Warning: Never tell an interviewer that your goal in life is to own your own business. Companies have a distinct aversion to hiring and training future competitors.

10. Do you have any questions? Can you think of anything else you would like to add?

It would be a mistake to answer "no" or to state that everything has already been thoroughly covered. Chances are that the interviewer omitted one or several critical areas that would strengthen your qualifications for the job. Even if nothing crucial was omitted, it is useful to go over again your strongest areas to demonstrate that you would be the most logical candidate for the opening.

If there were any relevant soft spots in your preceding interview, now is the time to cast the negative issues in a more positive light. While you can't make a silk purse out of a sow's ear, a bad interview can sometimes be turned around by countering all the negatives that may have emerged.

If the interviewer asks you whether you have any questions, don't answer in the negative. A negative answer may leave the impression that you're really not interested in the job. A better track is to ask some intelligent questions about the company and the opening that show how knowledgeable and up-to-date you are about the company and the industry in general. This, of course, presumés that you've done your homework and read the current trade magazines or professional journals that cover news about the companies in your field.

Responding to Negative Questions

When interviewing, never forget that employers don't hire candidates who complain, have negative attitudes, or reveal proprietary information about previous employers. Think about it. Would you rather work with someone who's positive or negative?

When Frank Bartlett (not his real name), a controller for a small manufacturing company, interviewed for a position as assistant division controller at a larger company, he wasn't aware that the larger firm was considering a joint venture with the smaller company. Asked what he liked least about his current employer, Mr. Bartlett showed an unfortunate lack of discretion. He responded to the negative question with a negative answer and revealed that his employer's financial affairs were being mismanaged and that the firm was in serious financial trouble. Not only did he not get the job, but he was laid off six months later after the joint venture was canceled.

"Interviewing is tough and intimidating, but when a candidate reveals confidential information, I immediately discount him or her," says Eric Notheisen, who works in staffing and administration for Martin Marietta's Astronautics Group in Englewood, Colorado. "Revealing such information clearly demonstrates a lack of integrity and common sense."

Everyone has negative experiences during their careers. From an employer's perspective, candidates who view these experiences positively are more in control of their lives. They're usually happier, more successful and productive, and better team players, managers, and leaders because others gravitate toward them.

Interviewers ask negative questions to determine whether or not you fit into this category. They want to identify any negative feelings you have about yourself, your performance, past employers, and business experiences. From your answers, they can flag personality traits and judge how you'll react to troublesome situations in the future.

Even experienced candidates can respond poorly to negative questions and expose feelings that may adversely affect their job prospects. The following suggestions will help you identify negative questions and respond in positive ways:

Don't Be Caught Off Guard

Many candidates don't adequately prepare for interviews, says Jean Marshall, manager of compensation and corporate human resources for Cyprus Minerals Company in Englewood, Colorado. Hence, they're often caught off guard by some questions and reveal negative circumstances or proprietary information to interviewers. "They instinctively say the first thing that comes to mind, and such responses often open the door for further probing of negative behavioral patterns," Marshall says.

To avoid being unprepared, review your career and make a list of negative experiences before interviewing. Then list the positive outcomes of those situations. What did they teach you? How did you grow? How did you turn the negative into a positive or cope positively with the issue? What did you do to improve the situation?

Unemployment is an obvious example of a negative career experience. Some positive aspects of joblessness might include having time to learn about yourself and plan your next career move, investigate other careers and industries, and reestablish contact with former business associates.

Some people view working in a highly stressful corporate culture as a negative situation. Through such an experience, though, you may have learned how to reduce the demands placed on your subordinates. You may also have learned how to effectively manage your stress level, remain productive, and help others cope with stress.

Working for a company with severe financial problems is another negative experience. Did you do anything that saved the company money? Did you increase your productivity? Did you learn how to better manage your personal finances? Did you learn what steps to take to avoid the situation at another company?

If you have negative feelings about a situation, you may have a hard time thinking of anything positive. In this case, ask an upbeat, objective friend or colleague to help you with your list.

Turn Negative Queries into Positive Statements about Your Candidacy

Open your mind to the fact that most negative experiences have positive aspects. Complainers dwell on life's negatives and have little good to say. They often act hurt or angry, blame others, and don't take responsibility for their actions. They either are avoided or push others away. They may be controlling and difficult to work with and often fail themselves and their employers. Don't fall into that trap.

After reviewing your career and completing your list of negative experiences, write down the ten to fifteen questions that would be most difficult for you to answer in an interview. Then, write answers to each question, reviewing them to make sure that they're positive. Practice your replies out loud, perhaps by asking a friend who's accustomed to conducting interviews to ask questions and evaluate your responses. Make your answers as spontaneous as possible or they will seem canned and over-rehearsed.

You'll usually recognize negative questions because they often include words such as *least, weakness, difficult, problems, conflict, politics,* and *criticism*. Some interviewers are more subtle, however. For example, Terry Gleason, vice president of human resources for Cyprus Minerals Company, uses positive phrases when asking negative questions. Typical queries might be: "If you could do anything different in your last job, what would it be?" or, "If you had the opportunity to get more training or education, what would it be in?" These provide insight into a candidate's strengths, weaknesses, learning, and growth potential, he says. "I need to know how a candidate will react in a variety of situations in this company," says Gleason. "An interviewer gets much better information from the candidate who turns a situation positive. It demonstrates how the person learns and grows."

The best strategy for answering a negative question is to lead the interviewer away from the negative issue and into the positive aspects. Your answer should be one to two minutes long and end on an upbeat note. Describe what you learned, how you grew professionally from the experience or how you turned a problem into an opportunity for the company and yourself. Note the good that came from the situation. Your goal is to demonstrate that you can effectively manage business situations and grow from the experience.

Learn from Negative Questioning

One final point: Candidates, too, can learn from negative questions. For example, if the majority of the questions you're asked are negative, you may be interviewing with a negative person or with a company that promotes a negative culture.

In most cases, a negative hiring manager will be a negative boss. If offered a job, ask yourself if you want to work with this person in such an environment. The answer is usually no.

Questions to Ask the Interviewer

At the close of most interviews, employers open the stage for you to ask questions. The table is turned at this point: You have been providing answers to the interviewer's questions for the first portion of the interview, and now it is your opportunity to get answers to any questions you have. Be careful, however, because the age-old saying "There is no such thing as a stupid question" does *not* apply to this scenario.

Your questions should be appropriate and well informed. For example, you should not ask questions about the company that were answered in the company's literature found at your school's career center or library. Asking a question like this shows that you did not adequately prepare for the interview or conduct any preinterview research. Likewise, questions about salary and benefits are not appropriate for this phase of the interview process. Asking those types of questions will lead you out the door instead of getting asked back for a second interview or an office visit. A bad question at the end of an interview can have a greater effect than all of the good responses you provided during an interview.

Instead, your questions should be job-related. Asking educated questions about the industry, the company, and/or the job itself will prove to the employers that you have done your research and you are truly interested in a career with their business.

Have a list of questions written out before you enter the interview. This list will show that you are prepared and it will ensure that you don't forget to ask something important. Here are some suggested questions to ask an interviewer.

- What qualifications do you think are most important for this job?
- What are the career opportunities in this organization for people who start in this position?

- Does the company have a training program? How long does it last?
- How are the job assignments determined at the end of the training program?
- Into what markets does the company expect to expand?
- What are your company's biggest challenges?
- What are some examples of the best results produced by people in this job?
- What are the company's future plans and goals?
- What exactly would you like to have me accomplish in this position?
- Will you be asking me to relocate?
- How soon do you expect to fill this position?
- How many people are you interviewing?
- Do you have any questions about my qualifications?
- Do you feel that this position is more analytical or more people-oriented?
- What criteria are used in performance evaluations? How frequent are they?
- What is the normal daily routine for this position?
- What is the average age of your first-level supervisors?
- What is the average age of top management?
- Is the sales growth in the new product line sustainable?
- What are your growth projections for the next three years?
- Have you had staff cutbacks in the last three years?
- Has there been much turnover in this job?
- May I talk with someone who held this position recently?
- Do you fill positions from the outside or promote from within?
- In what ways is a career with your company better than one with your competitors?
- Do you know _____ [your contact in the company]? (Make sure you check with that contact before you use his or her name.)

Prove It!

Hiring a new employee is a big investment and a big risk for any employer. After all, they are simply going on your word that you will provide the services that you claim you will be able to provide. You want employers to walk away from the interview feeling comfortable that an employment offer extended to you is the best decision they could possibly make.

How can you do that? You must *prove* to that employer that you are truly the best candidate for the position. Past performance is the best indicator of future performance. Therefore, you want to establish your track record by giving concrete examples of your past accomplishments and success. These concrete examples should include specifics so the employer can quantify the value you can provide. Relate your past experiences to the qualifications of the job for which you are interviewing. Proving it will not be that difficult when you follow these procedures:

1. Present a concrete example. Select a good "story."
2. Quantify. Include data: numbers, percents, frequency, volume per week/month/year.
3. Emphasize results. What happened as a result? (Increased profit, decreased turnover, improved productivity, solutions to problems, etc.)
4. Link it up. Tell the employer you can do it in this job too!

The Art of Storytelling

Aloof as they may seem, employers actually are begging you to get them excited. Show that you can make or save them money, solve their operational problems, or ease their workloads and they'll be thrilled to hire you. Merely saying you can increase productivity or get staff members to work as a team isn't enough. You must support your claims with vivid examples.

Using anecdotes to describe job skills is an infrequently used, but highly effective, interview technique. In less than three minutes, you can tell a powerful story that will make interviewers remember you favorably for days, weeks, or even months after a meeting. Interviewers have been known to track down people who have interviewed months ago for a job simply because they told such impressive stories about their previous accomplishments.

Interviewers prefer to hear "concrete examples of how people perform in real-life situations," says Bill Simons, human resources director of Microrim, a software company in Redmond, Washington.

"The greatest impact occurs when the accomplishment is one I can relate to, and is similar to situations that might be faced on the job," adds Tim Ainge, chief financial officer of U.S. West Paging in Seattle.

Sometimes, applicants are asked to describe their achievements in detail. The resulting stories can provide real insight into their abilities, says Sharon Smith, a personnel representative with Hewlett Packard in Palo Alto, California.

"The best candidates give plenty of information about what they can do for me," says Paul Green, a management consultant with Behavioral Technology in Memphis, Tennessee, who developed Hewlett Packard's interview system. "Stories must have a point that will showcase the candidate's skills."

Aim for Maximum Impact

A well-told story can mean a job offer instead of a rejection letter, says Green. "I was interviewing a plant manager and needed confirmation that the individual had a strong commitment to task completion," he says. "The candidate described a time when he had his appendix removed on a Thursday and was back in the office on Monday—to the shock of everyone at the plant. This story provided very strong evidence that he was a driven, hard-working person. He got the job."

Such lively anecdotes create strong visual images that remain with hiring managers. Thus, you should concentrate on imprinting employers' minds during an interview with pictures of your excellent performance in relevant work situations. A good way to do that is to use the "features, accomplishments, benefits," or FAB approach, says Stephen Shaw, an executive recruiter with ExecuSearch in Bellevue, Washington. Whenever you relate a story to interviewers, describe features of your personality that helped you succeed, what exactly you accomplished, and how your work benefited your employer.

Be sure to explain thoroughly, yet concisely, how you achieved results, advises John Prumatico, human resources director at Microsoft Corporation in Redmond, Washington.

The results you claim should be tangible or quantifiable, adds Lou Atler, partner with CJA Associates, an executive search firm in Tustin, California. A result that's not "anchored" in this way may be believed, but it won't be remembered, he says.

As a positive example, Atler cites a financial-planning director who said in an interview that one of his strengths was breaking through barriers. The director went on to describe a time when a profit-planning system he expected to implement quickly was threatened by a division president who was dragging his heels. To convince the division president to support his efforts, the director called to say he was going to fly more than a thousand miles just to spend fifteen minutes with him. A few days later, the trip became unnecessary when the embarrassed division president agreed to cooperate. This "anchor" convincingly demonstrated the financial-planning director's problem-solving skills.

Choose Stories Carefully

Selecting the right stories to tell will improve your interview success considerably. Begin by listing any work, hobby, sports, school or volunteer activities that you've performed well or enjoyed. Write down everything that pops into your mind until you have a list of thirty or more accomplishments. Examples of statements to include on such lists are:

- I received a $600 award from my employer for suggesting a money-saving idea.
- I earned my way through college by painting houses.
- I created a plan for flextime that reduced absenteeism.
- I implemented a just-in-time system that cut inventory 55 percent.
- I increased sales in my territory 36 percent in two years.
- I learned Russian so I could read *War and Peace* in the original language.
- My employer used my MBA thesis research and saved more than $30,000 in the first year.
- As fund-raising chairperson, I set a new record for donations.

Once your list is complete, review each accomplishment and visualize the events for at least one minute. Then take ten of your top accomplishments (work-related achievements are usually the best) and write 100 to 200 words about each one. Relive the experience and put your thoughts on paper, writing as fast as you can without worrying about spelling, grammar, sentence structure, or style. Describe the challenges you faced.

Next, practice describing your accomplishments. Strive to create strong images, and keep honing your delivery until you say exactly what you want. For maximum flexibility, develop a very tight one-minute version, and a longer three-minute one. Then, look for ways to weave these stories into your interviews, so that about a third of your responses contain vivid examples. When other candidates become a mere blur, your stories will stick out in hiring managers' minds and get you job offers you wouldn't have received otherwise. **Caution:** Tell *stories* not fairy tales!

Final Checklist

Do:

Allow time to fill out applications before the interview.
Practice questions and answers with a friend or relative.
Bring your résumé, letter of recommendation, other documents.
Take time to complete the application form carefully and neatly.
Learn as much as you can beforehand about the company.
Be certain that you can do the work for which you are applying.
Listen carefully; be polite and tactful.
Arrive five to ten minutes ahead of your appointment.
Be aware of your nonverbal communication.
Have your papers arranged for easy reference.
Always be positive and self-confident.
Be courteous to everyone you meet at the interview site.
Let your eye contact say, "I like you."
Be aware of your posture.
Make use of the first five minutes to sell your skills.
Wait until you are invited to be seated.
Look alert and interested at all times.
Answer questions honestly, accurately, briefly.
Be able to give a continuous record of your jobs.
Speak with confidence and enthusiasm.
Show proper respect for interviewer and secretary/receptionist.
Select your words carefully.
Stress your qualifications for the job and your interest in it.
Let the employer take the lead in the conversation.
Be realistic if you are asked to discuss wages.
Follow up job interviews immediately with a letter.
Make arrangements to call employer about a hiring decision.
Ask if more information is needed at the end of the interview.
Ask questions about the company and the position.
Be sure to thank the interviewer for his/her time.

Don't:

Worry about being nervous. That is usually expected.

Take anyone with you to your job interview.

Be negative.

Smoke or chew gum.

Schedule more job interviews a day than you can handle.

Argue with the interviewer.

Interrupt the interviewer.

Mention personal, home, or money problems.

Talk too much.

Criticize others, including past employers or co-workers.

"Beat around the bush" or "bluff" an answer.

Talk about money until you are offered the job.

Be too friendly and treat the interviewer like a "pal."

Be afraid to ask what you need to know.

Say, "I really need this job."

Become discouraged if your first interview doesn't go well.

Decorum

During an interview, prospective employers may also be observing your behavior, speech, mannerisms, and so forth for signs of propriety and good taste. Be aware of the impression you may make in the following ways:

The Handshake

Positive	Negative
Firm grip but not too strong	Weak
About one arm's length away	Sweaty palms
Hold for about 10 seconds	Iron grip
Greet employer while shaking hands	Challenging
	Pump arm excessively
	Too close
	Hold for too long

Nonverbal Communication

Positive	Negative
Maintain good eye contact	Staring or looking at ground
Smile when appropriate	Nervous giggling
Good posture	Slouching
	Hand twisting, overuse of hand gestures

Verbal Communication

Positive	Negative
Speak clearly and articulately	Mumbled
Not too fast and not too slow	Too fast or too slow
Be professional	Too casual
Proper grammar and pronunciation	Incorrect grammar and pronunciation
	Overemotional

Personality

Positive	Negative
Enthusiastic and motivated	Unresponsive
Genuine and sincere	Artificial
Decisive	Noncommittal
Responsible	Overbearing
Self-reliant	Excessively nervous

Tips from On-Campus Recruiters

On-campus recruiters have seen a thing or two in their days of visiting campuses across the nation. They probably have a few war stories that they can share about their experiences. Based on these experiences, they offer some tips to remember when interviewing. Pay special attention to their advice. After all, they are the experts on who and what on-campus recruiters are looking for.

Research organizations in advance of interviews. Since most on-campus interviews are relatively short, it is important that you use this time to sell yourself to an employer. Don't waste this opportunity by spending too much time on issues that could have been answered by reading the company's literature and/or by viewing its videotape. Displaying your knowledge about a potential employer will greatly enhance your chances of interview success.

Define your career goals and the opportunities you want. One of the keys to making a successful sale is product knowledge. In the case of job interviews, that product is *you*. You need to perform a thorough self-evaluation well in advance of your interviews. Know what your strengths, weaknesses, skills, and abilities are and be prepared to discuss them in the interview.

Be enthusiastic and sincere during your interviews. It is important for you to convey a genuine sense of interest during the interview. You must appear eager and flexible but not too rehearsed. Don't fixate on being nervous. Even seasoned pros can have the "interview jitters." Above all, *never* be late for an interview appointment.

Be honest. Don't claim interest in an employer if you really do not intend to work for that organization. Don't lie on your résumé or during the interview. Although you should never draw attention to your weaknesses, don't attempt to hide a shortcoming by being untruthful. Learn how to deal with perceived (or real) weaknesses *before* your interviews by talking to a campus career services professional and/or reading books on job interviewing techniques.

Be realistic. Carefully evaluate what an employer has to offer you—and what you have to offer the employer. Don't accept a position that isn't suited to you "just because you need a job." Although most entry-level salaries have been on the rise, do not set your starting salary expectations too high. If a starting salary seems inordinately low but is for a position that you really want, you might be able to arrange for an early salary review.

Types of Interviews

As a job applicant, you may encounter different types of interviews. Learning to recognize the various formats may help you do your best in each situation. Some of the most common interviews are screening, one-on-one, stress, panel and behavioral interviews, and an interview involving a site visit.

Screening Interview

This is a very formal interview that will occur during the first stage of the interview process. The interviewer is usually a human resources representative who is very well trained. The type of interview questions asked will be designed to gather specific information and will be asked of every applicant interviewing for that position in order to narrow down the applicant pool.

One-on-One Interview

This is the most common type of interview. The interviewer is usually a hiring supervisor and may not be very well trained as an interviewer.

Stress Interview

In this case the interviewer's goal is to make you feel uncomfortable, perhaps by avoiding eye contact, acting somewhat uninterested, or writing the entire time. Be aware of stress and expect it during the interview. Always maintain your composure during a stress interview situation.

Panel Interview

This is another form of the stress interview. You are interviewed by several interviewers who are familiar with various aspects of the job and the organization. It is very important to relax and maintain good eye contact. Be sure to pace yourself, since questions may come to you in a very rapid manner. Companies use panels because they provide a broad perspective in the hiring process and are helpful in building rapport. People who do well verbally and enjoy performing do best in the panel interview.

Behavioral Interview

This involves a structured pattern of questions designed to probe the applicant's past behavior in situations similar to those on the job. Behavioral interviews are based on the premise that the best predictor of future behavior or performance is past behavior or performance in similar circumstances. You can't bluff your way through a behavioral interview, because the open-ended questions are designed to determine whether you possess necessary qualities to do the job.

Site Visit

Candidates who have already been interviewed may be invited to a company location for a tour and additional interviewing.

The behavioral interview and the site visit are explained more fully in the next sections.

Are You Ready for a Behavioral Interview?

"Tell me about a time when you were on a team, and one of the members wasn't pulling his or her weight." If this is one of the leading questions in your job interview, you could be in for a behavioral interview. Based on the premise that the best way to predict future behavior is to determine past behavior, this style of interviewing is gaining wide acceptance among recruiters.

Today, more than ever, every hiring decision is critical. Behavioral interviewing is designed to minimize personal impressions that can affect hiring decisions. By focusing on the applicant's actions and behaviors, rather than subjective impressions that can sometimes be misleading, interviewers can make more accurate hiring decisions.

Behavioral vs. Traditional Interviews

If you have training in or experience with traditional interviewing techniques, you may find the behavioral interview quite different in several ways:

- Instead of asking how you would behave in a particular situation, the interviewer will ask you to describe how you did behave.
- Expect the interviewer to question and probe (think of "peeling the layers from an onion").
- The interviewer will ask you to provide details and will not allow you to theorize or generalize about several events.
- The interview will be a more structured process, which will concentrate on areas that are important to the interviewer, rather than allowing you to concentrate on areas that you believe are important.
- Most interviewers will be taking copious notes throughout the interview.

The behavioral interviewer has been trained to objectively collect and evaluate information and works from a profile of desired behaviors that are needed for success on the job. Because the behaviors a candidate has demonstrated in previous similar positions are likely to be repeated, you will be asked to share situations in which you may or may not have exhibited these behaviors. Your answers will be tested for accuracy and consistency.

If you are an entry-level candidate with no previous related experience, the interviewer will look for behaviors in situations similar to those of the target position:

"Describe a major problem you have faced and how you dealt with it."

"Give an example of when you had to work with your hands to accomplish a task or project."

"What class did you like the most? What did you like about it?"

Follow-up questions will test for consistency and determine if you exhibited the desired behavior in that situation:

"Can you give me an example?"

"What did you do?"

"What did you say?"

"What were you thinking?"

"How did you feel?"

"What was your role?"

"What was the result?"

You will notice the absence of such questions as, "Tell me about your strengths and weaknesses."

How to Prepare for a Behavioral Interview

Recall recent situations that show favorable behaviors or actions, especially involving course work, work experience, leadership, teamwork, initiative, planning, and customer service. Prepare short descriptions of each situation, so that you can give details if asked.

Be sure each story has a beginning, a middle, and an end, that is, be ready to describe the situation, your action, and the outcome or result. The outcome or result should reflect positively on you (even if the result itself was not favorable). Be honest, however; don't embellish or omit any part of the story. The interviewer will find out if your story is built on a weak foundation.

A possible response, for example, to the question, "Tell me about a time when you were on a team and a member wasn't pulling his or her weight" might be: "I had been assigned to a team to build a canoe out of concrete. One of our team members wasn't showing up for our lab sessions or doing his assignments. I finally met with him in private, explained the frustration of the rest of the team, and asked if there was anything I could do to help. He told me he was preoccupied with another class that he wasn't passing, so I found someone to help him with the other course. He was not only able to spend more time on our project, but he was also grateful to me for helping him out. We finished our project on time, and got a 'B' on it."

The interviewer might then probe with one or more of these questions: "How exactly did you feel when you confronted this person?" "Exactly what was the nature of the project?" "What was his responsibility as a team member?" "What was your role?" "At what point did you take it upon yourself to confront him?" You can see it is important that you not make up or "shade" information and why you should have a clear memory of the entire incident.

Use the Behavioral Questions Worksheet to help you with the details you might relate in answer to behavioral interview questions. Then study the list of behavioral interviewing questions to get you thinking about past behavior that employers may be interested in.

Behavioral Questions Worksheet

Planning and organizing

How were you able to balance your school work with extracurricular activities?

Activities

How balanced?

Result

Describe a situation at _____ that required you to accomplish several things at one time. What did you do?

Situation

Action

Result

Initiative

Have you suggested any new ideas to any of your bosses? What prompted the ideas? What happened?

Idea (suggestion)
Why suggested?
Result

Have you found any ways to make your job easier? Examples.
Situation
Action
Result

Motivational Fit

The extent to which people must work together closely varies from job to job. When have you been satisfied/dissatisfied with how closely you've had to work with others? Why?

Situation
Action
Satisfied/Dissatisfied

Customer Service Orientation

How frequently do (did) you have interactions with customers (internal/external) in your part-time job? Tell me about one of those interactions.

Situation

Examples of Behavioral Interview Questions

Judgment/Problem Solving

- Recall a time when your education and experience did not prepare you for a task. What did you do?
- Describe a problem you've recently been asked to solve.
- Give me an example of a good decision you have made recently.

Teamwork/Collaboration

- Interacting with others can be challenging at times. Describe a situation when you wished you had acted differently with someone.
- Describe a situation when you were able to help a team member or peer.
- Describe the best/worst team of which you have been a member.

Initiative

- Have you found any ways to make your job easier?
- Give me an example of your doing more than was required in your current job/class.
- Can you think of some projects or ideas (not necessarily your own) that were sold, implemented, or carried out successfully because of your efforts?

Adjustment/Flexibility

- Tell me about a difficult situation you recently had to manage.
- Jobs differ in the extent to which unexpected changes can disrupt daily responsibilities. How do you feel when this happens?
- Describe a situation that required several things to be done at the same time.

Leadership

- Tell me about a time when you were a leader.
- Describe a situation in which your efforts influenced the actions of others.

Planning and Organizing Work Management

- Walk me through yesterday (or last week) and tell me how you planned the day's (or week's) activities.

- Tell me about a time when your course load was heaviest. How did you get all of your work done?
- How were you able to balance your schoolwork with extracurricular activities/work?

Technical/Professional Knowledge

- Sometimes complex projects require additional expertise. Describe a situation when you had to request help or assistance with one of your projects or assignments.
- Describe how you've gone about learning a new technical skill.
- Describe a time when you solved a technical problem.

Customer Focus

- When you think of companies that serve their customers well, which companies come to mind? Why?
- Can you describe a situation in which you were able to "win over" a difficult customer?
- What is good customer service? How have you given good customer service?

Motivational Fit

- When were you most satisfied/dissatisfied in your work (school)? What was the most satisfying/dissatisfying about that?
- Tell me about a time when you had a lot of challenge in your work. How satisfied were you with that and why?
- Jobs differ in the extent to which people work independently or as part of a team. Which do you prefer? Why? Tell me about a time when you enjoyed working this way.

The Second Interview or What Is a Site Visit?

Many of your interviews may take place on campus with recruiters who visit from various companies. If the on-campus interviewer thinks you might be a good match for the job and the organization, the company may ask you to a second interview.

Private businesses often use a site visit to complete the college recruiting contact established on campus. Those students who are of greatest interest to the employer are invited for a further interview at the home office, district, or other plant locations. Site visit is *not* a guarantee of a job offer, however.

The site visit is a business experience, and students taking such trips should regard them as such. You should accept visit offers *only* if you have a reasonable interest in the employer. Your time is valuable, and a company's expenditure of money and time on such visits is sizable.

Prepare for your visit. Fill out any necessary application forms. Dig out as much information as you can about the company. Plan your wardrobe and be prepared for a long day.

The majority of site visit invitations are made by letter within two to five weeks after a campus interview. Employers may invite you to visit them over a semester break or extend the invitation during the semester. You may request another time if the one suggested is not convenient; the employer may or may not be willing to make other arrangements. Remember that site visits are not excused absences from class. You will need to discuss your plans with your professors.

Some employers, like some students, do a much better job than others with the site visit. Many companies handle your visit completely. That is, you are met at the airport by a representative, taken to your hotel, and given a tour of the community. Dinner and an evening's entertainment may be included. The employer sends a representative to the hotel the next morning to pick you up. Following the day's visit, you are then delivered to the airport. This is the *complete treatment*. With another company, however, you may be required to get to the motel on your own where you will find a packet of information telling you how to proceed to the location—on your own—the next day. Following the visit, your departure may also be on your own. Be prepared for either situation. If you are to be met, the employer usually gives you this information in advance, telling you by whom, where, and when.

There is a great deal to accomplish during a visit. Here are some things to consider:

1. Positions of responsibility occupied by recent graduates: How have recently hired graduates done? Are graduates just a few years older than you holding important positions? Does there seem to be an air of "progress" in the organization for younger graduates? It is not always easy to determine this in an organization, but you should attempt to find answers to these questions.

Chapter 9   Interviewing and Following Up

2. What impression do the physical facilities give you? Does the company have the latest and best equipment in the field, or are they just getting by with older equipment? What is the general level of plant maintenance?

3. What are the opportunities for further education in the community? Is there a university nearby? What is the reputation of the public school system?

4. How do you (and your spouse) feel about the location? Is it the type of area you want to live in? Can you afford to live there?

   One note about the final point: Each year career centers hear from many graduates—often within the first year of employment—who want to relocate because they dislike a given location. Much of this turnover could be avoided if new employees took more care in analyzing their own requirements. So think about it carefully! And remember: If you are working for a company with offices in several cities, sooner or later you may face relocation. You will be promoted (you certainly hope), and this frequently involves a move.

Expenses

The employer expects to pay for all legitimate expenses in connection with a site visit. "Legitimate expenses" are defined as those that are necessary to get you there and back, covering the basic items of transportation, food, and lodging. Be sure to keep all receipts to turn in to the company's accounting office for reimbursement.

Reimbursable expenses do *not* include the following items: personal entertainment or "side trips"; personal phone calls, except in emergencies; show or athletic tickets; alcoholic beverages, cigarettes, magazines; expenses for persons other than the individual invited on the site visit, except where the company authorizes expenses for the applicant's spouse.

Airfare: Most employers favor coach airfare for their own employees traveling on company business. We recommend that you use coach fare in the absence of employer instructions to the contrary.

Car rental: At times it may be necessary for you to use a rental car to reach an employer's location. If so, we recommend you use a moderately priced vehicle.

Food: Employers expect you to eat adequate meals, and most are quite liberal in this respect. But, if you have a choice between a

$15.00 steak and a $20.00 steak, we think you would be smart to choose the $15.00 one.

Lodging: Many employers make reservations for you in advance. If the employer does *not* offer to make your reservations, the same principle of adequate accommodation, but at a reasonable rate, should be observed.

Prorating expenses: If you visit two or more employers in the same city or general vicinity, it is proper to split the total cost of your visit equally between the employers visited. Each employer should be advised of your situation.

Your follow-up to a site visit should include a thank-you letter for the time and effort the company spent. Include favorable remarks about the facilities, employees, products, or services, based on what you saw and experienced.

Interview Follow-up: What It Is and Why It's Needed

The practice of following up a personal interview cannot be stressed too strongly. Follow-up basically means that within one to two days of your interview, you prepare and send a personal note of thanks (normally typed) to the person(s) who interviewed you. The basic points to be made are:

1. Your thanks for the opportunity to interview for the position.
2. Some of the things you feel make you a suitable/qualified candidate.
3. Your interest in hearing from him or her.

Writing a follow-up indicates that you are courteous, knowledgeable about the job search process, still interested in the position, and that you have thought further about the matchup between the employer's needs and your background.

Even though you may not be offered the position interviewed for, the impression a follow-up letter makes on the interviewer is usually very positive and can lead to employment with the same firm or organization at a later date or with another firm by referral. It is worth the time and effort involved.

Thank-You Letter Format

Street
City, State, ZIP
Date

Name of person, position
Company Name
Street or P.O. Box
City, State, ZIP

Dear _____:

First Paragraph. In this paragraph, thank the person for the opportunity to interview and explore the position further.

Second Paragraph. Review some of your personal attributes/background that you feel make you qualified for the position. You may also want to indicate further interest in the position. (If you feel that you are no longer interested in being considered, mention this here and formally withdraw yourself as a candidate.)

Third Paragraph. Generally express an interest in hearing from the interviewer(s) regarding your candidacy. You may want to indicate that you'll call on a certain date to check on things.

Closing,

Signature

Name (Typed)

Sample Thank-You Letter

1635 East 53rd Street
Chicago, IL 60615
June 9, 20xx

Janet Dowd
Director of Social Services
St. Joseph's Hospital
1234 Main Street
Chicago, IL 60636

Dear Ms. Dowd:

I enjoyed meeting with you last week to discuss the exciting opportunity in the play therapy program. St. Joseph's Hospital has certainly taken the lead in this important area, and I would be pleased to be associated with the program.

Our conversation further convinced me that a good match exists between my background and your expectations for the job. In addition to my major in psychology at DePaul University and the experience I have had in program development for the Chicago Department of Parks and Recreation, I would like to emphasize my participation in the project with Dr. Stein at Michael Rees Hospital. The experience provided me with insight into using dance as an effective mode of expression with certain groups of children, a concept I would like to develop further in the program at St. Joseph's.

I look forward to hearing from you soon. I can be reached during the day at (316) 555-1019. I will contact you by Friday if you are unable to reach me before then.

Sincerely,

Carla Fried

Carla Fried

Dealing with Rejection in the Job Search

After meticulously preparing your cover letters and résumés, you've sent them to carefully selected companies that you are sure would like to hire you. You've even had a few job interviews and followed all the right steps, before, during, and after them. Thanks, but no thanks. Your self-confidence melts and you begin to question your value to an employee.

Sometimes, we begin to dread the Big No so much that we stop pursuing additional interviews, thereby shutting off our pipeline to the future. We confirm that we couldn't get a job because we stop looking. Remember that fear of rejection doesn't have to paralyze your job search efforts. Let that fear fuel your determination; make it your ally and you'll learn a lot.

Eight Guidelines to Ward Off Rejection

1. **Depersonalize the interview.** Employers may get as many as 500 résumés for one job opening. How can you, I, and the other 498 of us be no good?

2. **Don't make it all or nothing.** Don't set yourself up for a letdown: "If I don't get this job, I'm a failure." Tell yourself, "It could be mine. It's a good possibility. It's certainly not an impossibility."

3. **Don't blame the interviewer.** Realize interviewers aren't in a hurry to think and behave our way. If you blame your turndown on a stone-hearted interviewer who didn't flatter you with beautiful compliments, you will learn nothing.

4. **Don't live in the past.** When you dredge up past failures, your nervous system kicks in and you experience all the feelings that go with failure. Unwittingly, you overestimate the dangers facing you and underestimate yourself.

5. **Don't get mad at the system.** Does anything less pleasurable exist than hunting for a job? Still, you must adjust to the world rather than make the world adjust to you. The easiest thing is to conform, to do what 400,000 other people are doing. When you sit down to play bridge or poker or drive a car, do you complain about the rules?

6. **Take the spotlight off yourself.** Sell your skills, not yourself. Concentrate on what you're there for: to find out the interviewer's problems and to show how you can work together to solve them.

7. **See yourself in a new role.** Form a mental picture of the positive self you'd like to become in job interviews, rather than focusing on what scares you. Before you can effect changes, you must really "see" yourself in the new role.

8. **Maintain your sense of humor.** Nobody yet has contracted an incurable disease from a job interview.

▲ Conclusion

You wouldn't enter an important athletic event without practicing; the same is true for your job interview. This chapter provided a wealth of information and tips for a successful interview, but the only way to truly be prepared for an interview is to practice.

▲ Activity

Visit your career center or academic advisor and ask for assistance. Explain that you are preparing for your job search and you want to gain some experience in interviewing. Ask if there are local businesspersons who would be willing to conduct a mock interview with you. A mock interview is a real interview, but for a mock job.

The person conducting the mock interview will ask you typical interview questions, but at the end, they will provide you with suggestions for improvement. Ask your mock interviewer to grade your performance in the following areas: your preparation, personality, appearance, communication skills, and ability to articulate your experience and career goals. After the interview, don't forget to write that individual a thank-you letter. Not only is this a great way to practice writing such a letter, but it should show sincere appreciation for that person's time and commitment in helping you prepare for your job search.

Chapter 10
Using Technology in Your Job Search

INTRODUCTION

Technology is changing faster than most people can keep up with it. Today, the Internet is the fastest growing and most up-to-date method of sharing information. The Internet provides the job searcher with a wealth of opportunities. There are many Internet locations that focus entirely on the job search, including on-line job listings, information on résumé writing and interviewing, and sites where you can post your résumé for employers to review.

Chapter 6 discussed the importance of researching employers prior to an interview. The Internet is a great resource for doing this, and there are many advantages to using it. If you have a computer at home, you can access the Internet at any time of day. Also, the information you find on the Internet may be more recent than the annual reports or written documentation that is held at your campus career center or library. Finally, mentioning to an employer during your interview that you read the company's Web page proves to the employer that you are not intimidated by new technology and that you have the initiative to take advantage of computer resources. A company's Web page will typically include information on the company's mission, sales growth, recent trends, locations, employees, and so forth.

The Internet

The Internet takes the job search to a much larger scale. It opens doors that otherwise might not ever open to you. Let's face it, it's a big world and your contacts can't personally know everyone. Value your contacts, however, because they are the key in setting you apart from everyone else.

On the Internet you can investigate companies and positions, display your résumé, send résumés via e-mail, keep up with job market trends, get on mailing lists, and access *more* career development resources.

Why Use the Internet?

1. **Networking:** it is the world's largest network, so use it to your advantage.
2. **Current growth of on-line job listings:** As the Internet expands and grows, so does the number of resources for finding jobs.
3. **Around the clock availability:** The Internet is at your convenience; you don't have to work around someone else's schedule to use it.
4. **Broad geographic reach:** It provides leads for areas in which you do not have a network of personal contacts.
5. **Opportunity to demonstrate skills:** The fact that you are on the Internet demonstrates your familiarity with this new market area.
6. **Different access to information and resources:** You can get information from the Internet that you can't get anywhere else.
7. **Résumé posting:** It gives your résumé one more chance to shine for job recruiters.

"Surfing the 'net" won't replace a trip to the career center, the library, or talking to contacts, but it will *enhance* your visits there.

Job hunting on the information superhighway can be fun. It's like going to the library and getting lost browsing among the stacks. You'll set out with a goal in mind and stumble across half a dozen other paths to explore. In turn, these roads will provide you with more information and contacts than you expected.

Internet Options

Worldwide Web: There are thousands of "home pages" that offer job search assistance. A home page is a computer screen that gives information about organizations and offers direct links to other organization's home pages. There are also a number of on-line databases to aid your job search. These databases post job listings and take your résumé.

You could do a Web search using career-related keywords. But to get you started, this chapter contains some Web site addresses for your career search. (Please be aware that sites may have changed from the time this information was published.)

Career Counseling

The Catapult, Career Services Professionals Homepage
http://www.jobweb.org/catapult/catapult.htm

Job Web, The National Association of Colleges and Employers
http://www.jobweb.org

Getting Past Go: A Survival Guide for College Graduates
http://www.aegonsmg.com/getgo/

Resources for Researching Potential Employers

Federal Job Opportunities Bulletin Board
telnet<fjob.mail.opm.gov>

Open Market Commercial Sites Index
http://www.directory.net/

Government Documents

U.S. Government Documents
gopher://umslvma.umsl.edu/11/library/govdocs

Library of Congress
http://lcweb.loc.gov/

All State Employment Offices—By State
ftp://listserv-
    ftp.dartmouth.edu/pub/listserv/fedjobs/General/stateadr.txt

Remember to keep a record of the sites (or bookmark) and databases you have explored.

Job Hunting on the Internet

The Riley Guide, *a reference guide site and gateway*
http://www.dbm.com/jobguide/.rileyguide.com

Career Track, *a link to career/job sites*
http://www.careertrack.com/jindex.html

JOBTRAK Listings
http://www.jobtrak.com

Monster.com, *job listings*
http://www.monster.com:/

College Grad Job Hunter, *career search advice, summer job links*
http://www.collegegrad.com/

Career Web Sites

Job Web   *www.jobweb.org*

- Maintained by the National Association of Colleges and Employers
- Contains job postings, including internships, co-op positions, and federal jobs
- Ability to search for jobs by geographic region and field of work
- Information on graduate and professional schools
- "How-to" modules on writing résumés, interviewing, and sending correspondence
- A career planning segment with help in making career choices

Career Site   www.careersite.com

- Confidential candidate database in which employers are only told the individual's identity after the candidate grants his/her permission
- Variety of company profiles
- Each candidate's profile contains an overview of that individual's interests, qualifications, and skills

Job Smart   www.jobsmart.org/tools/career/spec-car.htm

- A large number of Internet links that provide the following information on a variety of careers:
  - Training and education required for the career
  - Potential salary earned
  - What type of work environment an individual will work in
  - Some links include personal stories from individuals working in the field
  - Advice for newcomers

The Career Key   www.ncsu.edu/careerkey/index.html

- Information on personality types and work environment types and the importance of matching these
- Includes a personality assessment, "The Career Key," which will help individuals to know themselves better
- Ability to match jobs with the personality assessment
- Information on principles of good decision making

Career City   www.careercity.com

- Listing of over 125,000 jobs
- Ability to post your résumé for employers to view
- A variety of self-help pages:
  - Résumé advice
  - Great answers for tough interview questions
  - Ten big job interview mistakes
  - Salary negotiation tactics

Career Magazine   www.careermag.com

- Ability to search the job openings database by geographic location, job title, and skills required

- Variety of employer profiles
- Daily news articles that will help in planning a career search
- A message board where individuals can network with others, generate job leads, share experience, and seek advice

Career Mosaic   www.careermosaic.com

- Ability to search the job database by industry
- Information on career opportunities abroad
- "CollegeConnection," a site specifically for recent college graduates looking for jobs or current college students looking for internships

Career Web   www.cweb.com

- Database of professional, technical, or managerial jobs
- "Career Inventory," an employment search readiness inventory that will help individuals discover if they are doing everything they can to obtain a job
- Helpful hints for preparing résumés and responding to job listings
- The "Career Doctor" who writes articles regarding the "people side of work"

CareerPath.com   www.careerpath.com

- Ability to search the want ads of the nation's leading newspapers
- Ability to search the employer database with information on featured employers
- Tips on finding the right job, preparing for the interview, and negotiating salary
- Ability to create an on-line résumé

America's Job Bank   www.ajb.dni.us

- Ability to search for jobs by title, keywords, and DOT codes
- Ability to link to state and other public employment service sites
- Ability to link to an employer's Web site via the job posting

Employment Contacts
www.adm.uwaterloo.ca/infocecs/CRC/manual/jobworksearch.html

- Tips on Internet sources and traditional methods of finding job openings

- Creative methods of marketing yourself, including preparing résumés and presenting your qualifications in an interview
- Information on starting your own business
- Tips on how to research employers and how to network

NationJob Network www.nationjob.com
- Easy to narrow down to a specific field
- Will send you job postings that match your profile for free

Recruiting-links.com www.recruiting-links.com
- Matches your areas of interest to a company or companies
- Allows you to search employment opportunities on the companies' Web pages

Jobbank USA* www.jobbankusa.com
- Search employer databases
- Submit résumés
- Learn about career fairs

E-Span, The interactive Employment Network: http://espan.com/ *(On-line employment connection)*

FedWorld: http://www.fedworld.gov/jobs/jobsearch.html *(Resource for U.S. Federal government jobs)*

Career Sites by Discipline

Physical Education, Health, Fitness, and Recreation

American Therapeutic Recreation Association http://www.atra-tr.org/ *(Jobs and info)*

Guide to WWWorld of Health and Sport Sciences: http://www.ithaca.edu/library/htmls/hshp.html *(Gateway links)*

Cool Works: http://www.coolworks.com/showme/ *(Jobs in recreation, national parks, cruises, resorts, etc.)*

*Member services employment advertising—requires a user name.

Online Sports Career Center:
http://www.onlinesports.com/pages/careercenter.html *(Job and résumé banks)*

American Alliance for Health/Physical Education, Recreation, and Dance: http://www.aahperd.org/ *(Jobs)*

NAIA News (National Association of Intercollegiate Athletes http://www.naia.org

NCAA's The Market: http://www.ncaa.org/market/ads *(Jobs)*

Peterson's Summer Camp Jobs:
http://careers.petersons.com/CJ$BldSrchForm.Summer_Jobs *(Find summer camp jobs by state)*

Social Service

Pysch Web: http://www.gasou.edu/psychweb/psychweb.htm *(Jobs and info)*

Mental Health Net: http://www.cmhc.com *(Jobs and info)*

Good Works: http://www.essential.org/goodworks/jobs/ *(Jobs)*

Social Work and Social Services Jobs Online:
http://gwbweb.wustl.edu/jobs/index.html *(Jobs and resources)*

Community Career Center: http://www.nonprofitjobs.org/ *(Database of jobs and employers)*

Peace Corp: http://www.peacecorps.gov/ *(Info and application, etc.)*

Sports-Related Job Listings and Résumé Bank

The Online Sports Career Center is a resource of sports-related career opportunities and a résumé bank for potential employers within the many segments of the sports and recreation industries. The Online Sports Career Center can be accessed at the following Web page: www.onlinesports.com/pages/careercenter.html. The Web page includes the following lings:

Job Bank

Find out about jobs in the sports and recreation industry. These are listed by sport, team, department, or suppliers of sports equipment.

Résumé Bank

You can post your résumé (ASCII text format online). Send e-mail to résumés@onlinesports.com.

Subscribe to National Sports Employment Newsletter

You can receive biweekly updates on new jobs in the sports and recreation industries.

Work with Online Sports

The Online Sports catalog for the Internet community.

Education

- Chronicle of Higher Education: http://chronicle.com/jobs/ *(Jobs in higher education)*
- Job Listings in Academia: http://volvo.gslis.utexas.edu/~acadres/jobs/index.html *(Academic jobs by state/inst.)*
- Teach for America: http://www.teachforamerica.org/ *(Applications and info)*
- U.S. Department of Education: http://www.ed.gov/EdRes/EdSupport.html *(Teacher's guide to the United States Department of Education)*
- American Mathematical Society: http://www.ams.org/careers/ *(Jobs and career info)*
- National Academic Advising Association: http://www.ksu.edu/nacada *(Info and jobs)*

Allied Health

- Mayo Online Career Center: http://www.mayo.edu/career/career.html *(Job listings)*
- Healthcare: http://www.medsearch.com/ *(Job listings)*
- National Athletic Trainers' Association http://www.med.und.nodak.edu/depts/sportmed/placemt/natapc.htm *(Jobs)*

Graduate and Professional Schools

- US News and World Report: http://www.usnews.com/usnews/edu/beyond/bcrank.htm *(Grad Ranking)*
- Graduate School Guide: http://www.schoolguides.com/ *(Guides to doctoral, master's and professional degree programs)*
- Petersons.com: http://www.petersons.com/graduate *(Grad school info)*

Association of American Medical Colleges:
http://www.aamc.org/ *(Medical school info)*

Yahoo: http://www.yahoo.com/health/medicine/education/medical_schools/ *(Medical school info)*

Medical School Interview Pages: http://www.interviewfeedback.com/ *(Interview info)*

Law School Admission Council: http://www./lsac.org/ *(Info)*

Yahoo: http://www.yahoo.com/government/law/law_schools/

GRE: http://www.gre.org/ *(Graduate Record Examinations info)*

GMAT: http://www.gmat.org/#textmenu *(Graduate Management Admissions Test info)*

Additional On-Line Help

Search Engines and Resources

AT&T Yellow Pages Directory: http://www.yellowwweb.com/ *(Business Directory)*

Big Book: http://www.bigbook.com/ *(Yellow pages directory)*

All in One: http://www.allonesearch.com/ *(Combines search engines, databases, indexes, and directories in a single site.)*

Alta Vista: http://www.altavista.digital.com/ *(Search engine)*

Yahoo: http://www.yahoo.com *(Search engine)*

Infoseek: http://www.infoseek.com *(Search engine)*

Research

Occupational Outlook Handbook: http://stats.bls.gov/ocohome.htm *(Occupational statistics)*

Bureau of Labor Statistics: http://stats.bls.gov/ *(Labor statistics)*

Hoover's Online: http://hoovweb.hoovers.com/ *(Company information)*

StreetLink Investor Information Center: http://www.streetlink.com/ *(Profiles on public corporations)*

Unique Career Resources

- Salary Calculator: If I earn $20,000 a year in Kalamazoo, how much will I need to earn in New York City to maintain my standard of living? Figure it out here! (http://www2.homefair.com/calc/salcalc.html)

- CityNet — Information on cities around the world, including maps (in any range of detail) when you type in a street address. (http://www.citynet.com/)

▲ Conclusion

As you can see, the Internet is a vast resource. If you have never accessed the Internet before, it may appear a bit intimidating. Once you get "on-line," however, you will realize just how simple it is. To prove this point, it is now time for you to get connected and start surfing the 'net.

▲ Activity

Refer back to chapter 2 where you wrote your job-search marketing plan. During that activity, you were to write some industries and some particular companies in which you are interested. Use this material to do your Internet search. See what information you can find regarding the industries that you are considering for a possible career. Also, look up the companies that interest you. Do they have Web sites? If so, what kind of information can you find on them that will assist you during your job search? Search some of the job listing Web sites. Are you able to find some available positions that appeal to you?

The Internet is a huge network of information that you should use to your benefit. Getting familiar with the Internet now will not only assist you in your job search, but can also be helpful for conducting research for your college courses. Use and enjoy!

Chapter 11
Gaining Professional Experience

INTRODUCTION

Many of you, as student-athletes, have participated in scrimmages. The purpose of a scrimmage is to prepare for a real game. It feels like the real thing and it looks like the real thing, but it is a way to test the waters and see if the team is truly prepared for the upcoming real thing.

The same can be said of internships, co-operative education, and summer employment. By participating in any of these activities, you are able to test the waters and see if you want to commit to a full-time career in that particular area. You can think of it as a scrimmage, a trial period, or a training ground. You will get to eat, sleep, and drink the real thing, without it being the real thing.

These activities are a great way for you to learn more about the industry or career that you are considering. You will get to experience "a day in the life" of someone in your field. This is a great opportunity to evaluate what you like and dislike about a certain career.

Besides the opportunity to learn more about the true world of work, internships, co-ops, and summer employment provide great experience that employers are seeking. Put yourself in an employer's shoes. If you were deciding between two equally qualified candidates and one person had done an internship gaining valuable experience and training, which would you choose for the job? An employer wants to hire someone who has "been there, done that"—someone who has a proven track record of success in the business world, someone who will not require a lot of training, someone with experience.

This chapter will fill you in on the details of internships and co-operative education. It will also provide tips on how to find these opportunities so you can acquire that much-sought-after experience.

Professional Experience Programs

Benefits

Professional experience programs offer you the chance to integrate classroom theory with career-related work experience. This work experience can enhance your classroom learning while you explore and clarify your career goals. Career-related work experience also increases your chances of finding satisfying employment upon graduation. Employers tell us they prefer candidates who have developed job-related skills and knowledge through career-related work experience. Perhaps most importantly, career-related work experience expands your network of professionals in your field of interest. This network becomes a valuable resource as you conduct your search for a full-time job.

Finding Opportunities

- Meet with the professional experience coordinator in your department.
- Meet with your career advisor in career services.
- Network with students in your department, alumni, faculty, members of professional organizations, and family and friends.
- Participate in career fairs.
- Visit the Career Center.
- Participate in on-campus interviews.
- Prepare your job-search materials.

Internships and Co-ops

An internship is typically a full-time, temporary work experience that is directly related to your field of study, career goal, or both. Some universities will grant course credit for internships, whereas others may not. You should meet with your advisor or a faculty member to discuss this issue. Internships may be paid or unpaid; they may be conducted during an academic year or in the summer. As you can see, there is a great deal of variety and flexibility associated with internships.

There are many advantages to an internship, including the potential for college credit and an above-market salary. Other advantages include the opportunity to experience the real world of work. This provides you the information you need to determine if the career you are interested in is truly a good fit for you. Also, internships provide valuable work experience that so many employers are seeking from job candidates. As an added bonus, many employers who hire interns will extend a full-time job offer to students who have performed well during the internship.

You should begin planning for an internship during or after your sophomore year. Internships are typically completed during the summer between the junior and senior year, but it is not unheard of to participate in an internship during the summer before your junior year. Most academic departments offer either required or elective internship programs.

Career-related experience is almost essential in today's tight job market. Experience in student organizations provides job transferable skills, but an internship provides more. An internship demonstrates:

- commitment to the career field
- initiative to pursue a goal
- ability to plan for the future and prepare accordingly
- knowledge of skills specific to the career field

Employers are looking for all these qualities. In addition, employers value the reduced training costs that accompany new hires with related experience.

One of the best ways to search for an internship is at your school's career center. The career center probably hosts employers who visit campus to interview for internship positions. Visiting the career center at the start of your sophomore year will ensure that you don't miss any important deadlines for this process. Also, the career center will have reference materials regarding internships and how you can find them.

The Internet, which you read about in the previous chapter, is also a great resource for finding internships.

A co-op, or cooperative education program, is similar to an internship in that it offers valuable, hands-on work experience and is directly related to your field of study, career goal, or both. One of the differences, however, is the fact that co-ops are typically conducted during multiple semesters or a summer plus an academic semester. One type of co-op involves alternating full-time semester of classroom study with full-time semesters of work assignments. Another form consists of simultaneous participation in full-time classroom study and a part-time work assignment for a co-op employer during consecutive semesters.

Because co-ops run for multiple semesters, students usually experience an increase in their work responsibility throughout the extent of the co-op. Also, by working for a company during different periods throughout the year, you are able to experience a greater part of the business cycle that is associated with that particular industry. An example of a typical co-op schedule follows:

	Fall	*Spring*	*Summer*
Freshman	School	School	School
Sophomore	School	Work	School
Junior	Work	School	Work
Senior	School	School	School

A co-op may prove more difficult for a student-athlete because of the required commitment to a multiple-semester work experience. Many companies are flexible, however, and you should not give up on this option until you have spoken with an advisor.

Students are paid for co-op work and generally receive course credit. Thus, cooperative education is a great way to assist in the expenses of paying for college. If you are interested in a co-op, you should visit with an advisor or career center staff member during your sophomore year. Keep in mind, however, competition is tough.

Getting Started

Applying for internships or cooperative education experiences will be your first chance to market yourself. Competition is tough, especially for summer internships. Academic standing and extracurricular involvement, especially leadership positions, weigh heavily in the selection process.

In order to take advantage of this opportunity, start researching internships and co-ops in your field and building a network of contacts.

The following are some questions to consider:

- Can you choose a specific area in your field for your internship? Do you want to limit yourself?
- How do students typically receive internships? Through the department or on their own?
- Who usually hires interns in your field? Federal government? State and local government? Large corporations? Nonprofit organizations? Self-employed individuals?

College advisors and other students in your field will have the most complete answers to these questions. Others who may be a source of assistance are: former students, professors, career planning and placement staff, academic supervisors, coaches, relatives, and acquaintances.

▲ Conclusion

As a student-athlete, you probably think you don't have the time to gain professional experience while attending school and participating in your sport. Your schedule is already stretched to its limits, right?

It will definitely be a challenge to incorporate an internship, cooperative education, or career-related summer employment into your busy schedule, but it will definitely be worth it. In fact, in a survey, one piece of advice that former college football players consistently mention is that current student-athletes should participate in an internship. There is no better way to gain experience or decide on the best career for you than to actually live it.

Talk to your coaches and advisors to see if they can assist you in the process. Consider creative ways to gain experience, such as part-time internships during the off-season. You never know what an employer might be willing to do for you until you ask. Make the most of your time in college, including summers. You will not have similar opportunities to test the waters in your future. Take advantage of it.

Chapter 12
Negotiating Salary and Benefits

INTRODUCTION

How much do you think you are worth? Will an employer have to pay you $30,000 for your first full-time job, or do you think you should earn $75,000 for that first year? The answer to this question is something that you will need to know before you interview and start to compare job offers extended to you from different companies. Many employers will ask you during the interview how much you feel you should be paid. Are you prepared to answer this type of question? If you aren't prepared, you may respond with a lower figure than what a company was willing to offer you and thus lose yourself a great deal of money. Preparation for this topic will require research and self-analysis.

If you are presented with multiple job offers, the choice is easy if you only weigh your alternatives based on salary. There are many other factors, however, that may influence your decision. For example, do you plan on continuing your education? If so, you may want to ensure that a company is willing to reimburse you for educational expenses. Are you relocating for your job? You may want to discuss relocation bonuses or reimbursement for relocation expenses. Is it important for you to start setting money aside for your retirement? If so, 401K plans and stock purchase options will be something of interest for you to research.

As you can see, there is a lot more involved when making a decision based on multiple job offers. Don't forget about vacation time, insurance, professional development, and work-related expenses. This chapter will provide you a basis on which to evaluate job offers. It will also assist you in gaining the skills needed to effectively negotiate salary or much-desired benefits. The time to negotiate for these items is before you accept the offer. Once you accept the offer and start work, your bargaining power drastically decreases. You need to be able to take advantage of this opportunity and guarantee that you are getting the most for your time and commitment.

Where to Find Salary Information

When considering a job offer or evaluating multiple job offers, you need to have some idea of the appropriate salary range for a given position. There are several sources of information about salaries. **Professional journals** are likely to publish articles or studies on compensation in their respective fields. **Professional associations** often conduct surveys of their members and might provide some information about salary ranges. The **help wanted ads** in newspapers and journals will sometimes list ranges for positions similar to the one you are considering, in a variety of geographic locations. The *Occupational Outlook Handbook*, the *American Almanac of Jobs and Salaries*, and other career books give approximate salary ranges.

Do remember, however, that the size of an organization can make a big difference. Large organizations may pay slightly more but have comparatively rigid salary scales and performance review schedules; small employers may reward outstanding performance more readily with bonuses and pay increases but may not offer the same employee benefits as a large employer.

Because of the differences from firm to firm, and industry to industry, your personal contacts can be a good source of information about salaries either within their own firms or within a particular industry or profession. Your career advisors will probably know the approximate salary schedules of some employers.

It is important to remember during your investigation that you are seeking an equitable range, not a definite figure.

Negotiating Your Compensation

Salary negotiation is the last step in the job search process. Generally, salary is determined by several criteria: your education, experience, previous offers, salary history, and the organization's needs. When your position is one that generates revenue, the amount of revenue it generates is often a factor in determining the salary.

Keep in mind that you should defer discussing salary and benefits until you have received a job offer. Once the employer has offered you a position, be sure you understand the salary and benefits package that is being offered to you. The time to negotiate is before you agree to the terms of employment. Once you have agreed to certain employment conditions, it may be very difficult for you to bargain for more.

A comprehensive discussion of salary and benefits includes:

- Compensation: salary and, when appropriate, commissions
- When and how work is evaluated (timing of performance appraisals and standards used to determine salary increases and bonuses)
- Health, retirement, and life insurance benefits
- Vacation, paid holidays, and sick time
- Administrative support: office; orientation and training; support staff; and resources such as consultants, computer hardware, and software
- Professional development: continuing education and training (e.g., tuition allowances, membership in professional associations, travel to conferences)
- Miscellaneous: expense account, clubs, moving/relocation costs
- Job-related expenses: travel, professional development, continuing education, conferences, professional publications. (If an employer cannot offer you a salary that meets your requirements, he or she may be able to offset some or all of the difference by covering job-related expenses that are usually absorbed by the employee.)

Questions you might consider asking regarding salary information include:

- What is the starting salary range in this company for this type of position?
- How often are salary and job performance reviewed?
- Does one have recourse if there is a disagreement about a review?
- What are the criteria used to get certain high salaries here?

- Is there a bonus plan, or are there stock options? How long before one is eligible to participate?
- Does this company have a profit-sharing plan with its employees? How long before one could participate in it?

Possible questions about benefits include:

- What percentage of medical and dental expenses are paid for by the insurance policy?
- What is the percentage of premiums paid by the employee for coverage?
- Does the policy cover parental leave?
- Is there disability income protection? How much? Under what conditions?
- What is the sick-leave policy?
- Is there a policy of personal-leave days?
- When does the vacation benefit begin?
- Are holidays paid vacation days also?
- Can I choose vacation days as I see fit to arrange for them with my family?
- Does the company have an educational or tuition reimbursement policy?
- Would I be permitted to attend professional conferences, seminars, and courses at company expense, with the approval of my immediate supervisor?
- Does the company provide any in-service educational programs?
- Does the company pay professional dues for its employees who belong to professional associations?

Weighing Compensation

Asking these kinds of questions about salary and benefits is part of the search preparation phase of the negotiation. Once the information has been gathered and all the questions have been answered to your satisfaction, you can evaluate the job's monetary limits as well as other aspects of job satisfaction and the personal value you attach to them. Then the negotiation begins. This is not the time to panic. Think. Be cool. Be professional about your deliberations. You have all the information on which to base counteroffers and with which to negotiate. The company has stated the salary or salary range. You must decide where your "turndown" point is and make sure that your personal job-satisfaction values are met.

Weighing the entire compensation package takes time but it will be well worth it in the end. Be patient and take the time to take care of yourself. Your greatest opportunity for negotiations is before you begin to work for a company. This is the only time you and the company's negotiator are on equal footing. Remember that, but don't be arrogant about it. On the other hand, don't shy away from the responsibility of taking care of yourself.

Salary Negotiation Strategies

- Never talk money until they decide they want you.
- Know, in advance, the probable salary range for similar jobs in similar organizations.
- If asked what salary you are looking for, bracket your salary range beginning with the company's probable offer and ending above what you will settle for
- Never say no to an offer before it is made, or within twenty four hours after.

Don't close the door to any possibility, that is, jumping to a conclusion. You need to go through the entire process and think it through.

Multiple Job Offers

How to Get Them and Tips on Managing Them

If you possess the technical skills in high demand today, recruiters say that you are likely to receive more than one job offer. Yes, even though many companies are still restructuring their management ranks (i.e., "downsizing"), they will continue to recruit college graduates because they need fresh talent to help their companies grow.

Besides having high-demand technical skills, graduates who receive multiple job offers are usually positive, inquisitive, and truthful:

1. **Be Positive.** "If you hate the interview process, it will come across," says Vicki Spina, career strategist and author of *Getting Hired in the '90s*. "You have to find at least one thing about the job search/interview process that you like—such as meeting people or getting to know the companies—and celebrate it."

2. **Be Inquisitive.** Recent graduate Paul Jones landed a job at Bosque Steel because he did his research and asked outstanding questions dur-

ing his interview. At a job fair, he visited Bosque's booth and spoke with a recruiter who told him there were no present job openings.

Jones struck up a conversation with the recruiter anyway, sharing his knowledge of the company with her. She was so impressed with him that one week later she called Jones about a job that had just opened. He interviewed and was offered the job of his dreams; one that provides the international experience he was looking for—and a salary of $10,000 more than what he had expected.

3. **Be Truthful.** Employers will like you better if you talk about both your strengths and weaknesses. When you open up to the employer about your weaknesses, it makes your entire conversation more believable and sincere. But once you bring up your weakness(es), be sure to tell the interviewer what steps you have taken to improve.

Weighing All the Factors

How do you choose which job is right for you? First, start by developing a "pros and cons" list for each job, says Spina. Make sure this list is all-inclusive. Think about the features of each, such as salary, benefits, corporate culture, commuting time, flexible work arrangements, tuition reimbursement, and on-the-job learning opportunities.

"Don't go for one offer just because it has better pay and benefits," says Spina. "Go for the one where you feel comfortable working in their environment. Money will not be enough a year from now if you hate the environment."

Determine what is really important to you. For most recent graduates, says Spina, educational assistance is important because many of them plan to seek higher educational degrees.

"If you are weighing offers and they are pretty equal down the line, this is where your gut feeling really comes into play. Look at your priorities and ask yourself what truly is important to you," says Spina.

Evaluating an Offer

For every potential position, you will want to carefully evaluate whether it will meet and advance your career goals and how it will fit with your other life commitments and priorities. The clearer you are about what you want, the better you will be able to determine if a potential position and employer are the best choice for you. Take the time to learn about both the position and the employer in order to make an informed decision. Compare what you have learned to your career goals. Is the job a good fit for you?

Never Burn Your Bridges

Keep in mind the importance of diplomacy when rejecting an offer, because in today's fast-paced work world, you never know when your work environment may shift or when your job may be eliminated.

Paul Siker, principal of the Guild Corporation in McLean, Virginia, offers this example for diplomatically declining an offer: "I really appreciate the offer, and although I feel another position I've been offered is a better fit for my goals, I really want to say how impressed I am with your company and how much I have enjoyed everyone I've had the opportunity to meet. Perhaps in the future, there will be something that's a better fit for both of us."

Responding to a Job Offer

When you receive a job offer from an employer, you will be expected to give your decision within a reasonable amount of time. The employer may indicate the date by which he or she expects to hear from you. If you need additional time to consider the offer, you might request that, using the type of letter shown in "Job Offer Letter—Delay Decision" in an example that follows.

The other examples show the format you might use if you choose to **decline** an offer or **accept** an offer. Whether you are accepting or rejecting an offer or asking for more time to decide, remain tactful, follow standard business letter style, and proofread your letter carefully. Above all, make sure your letter clearly states your intentions.

How to Choose among Multiple Job Offers— A Worksheet

1. Review the items (see p. 183) in Column 1 and add any other factors that you might use in deciding about a job.
2. In Column 2, check off the items that would influence your decision about a job offer.
3. Use Column 3 to prioritize the factors you've checked off; give each a letter. A=I must have this (most important); B=I really want this (important); C=This would be nice to have (least important).

WORKSHEET

Column 1	Column 2	Column 3
Fulfilling work		
Variety of work		
Responsibility		
Recognition		
Autonomy		
Challenge		
Advancement opportunity		
Schedule		
Working conditions		
Salary		
Fringe benefits		
Training program		
Location of job		
Commuting distance		
Company size		
Company reputation		
Friendliness of co-workers		
Evaluation system		
Other factors:		

Job Offer Letter—Delay Decision

Student Address
City, State, ZIP

Date

Contact Name
Contact Title
Company Name
City, State, ZIP

Dear Mr./Ms. Contact Last Name:

First paragraph: Express sincere appreciation for the job offer. Identify the position which you are considering. Indicate the amount of time you are requesting.

Second paragraph: Cover details of the offer you are considering, such as position duties/responsibilities, location, start date for employment, and agreed-upon starting salary.

Concluding paragraph: Reiterate your appreciation for the offer. Indicate the time period (for example, the week of July 22) you will call with a decision and how you may be contacted in the interim. Thank the employer for considering your request for additional time.

Respectfully,

Student Name

Job Offer Letter—Decline

Student Address
City, State, ZIP

Date

Contact Name
Contact Title
Company Name
City, State, ZIP

Dear Mr./Ms. Contact Last Name:

First paragraph: Express sincere appreciation for the job offer. Identify the position for which you were given an offer.

Second paragraph: State the reasons for refusing the offer, as related to your career goals and geographic preferences. Decline the offer explicitly.

Concluding paragraph: Thank the employer again for his or her time.

Respectfully,

Student Name

Job Offer Letter—Acceptance

Student Address
City, State, ZIP

Date

Contact Name
Contact Title
Company Name
City, State, ZIP

Dear Mr./Ms. Contact Last Name:

First paragraph: Express sincere appreciation for the job offer. Identify the position you are accepting.

Second paragraph: Cover necessary details such as the agreed-upon start date for employment, location, and starting salary.

Concluding paragraph: Indicate your enthusiasm about beginning your new job. Reiterate your appreciation for the offer.

Respectfully,

Student Name

Relocation: Should You Make the Move?

Relocation has become as much a part of professional life as fax machines and voice mail. Whether out of want or need, most employees will probably relocate at least once in their careers. Even the recent college graduate must think beyond the areas around home or school when looking for his or her first job.

It is helpful to realize just how radically the concept of a job or profession has changed. It wasn't long ago that a person chose a job in one location—and that was it. Many people, even those with a college education, spent their lifetimes in the same jobs because changing jobs was, in many cases, unthinkable. Leaving a job was often regarded as betrayal, and potential employers tended to be suspicious of those who had left (or wanted to leave) a secure position for one with another company.

In this increasingly mobile society, however, that perception has changed. It is common for professionals to move from one state to another, not only to new jobs but to new careers as well. So a first job out of college may be just that—start before it's time to move on. Keep that in mind as you gain experience in an entry-level position.

If you decide that relocation is for you, or you feel it is necessary because of the state of your local job market, consider the logistics before hitting the road. First of all, what is your salary in relation to living expenses? Someone living on $24,000 a year in a small town will have a tough time making it on the same amount in New York City.

Yet the reverse also can be true. Someone from a big city may overlook the fact that a modest salary in a less populated area might add up to more disposable cash because housing, food, and other expenses may not be as costly in a smaller area. If you are fortunate enough to have the luxury of choosing between offers in different cities, be sure to factor in the comparative costs of living.

Consider, too, those close to you. If your spouse works, under what circumstances could he or she make the same kind of move? Could you pull your children out of a school or day-care center you like? Even single candidates might have to discuss moving with a significant other.

Transportation is another factor. A large metropolis might offer efficient public transportation; a more suburban area could mean the need for a car and the monthly payments and insurance premiums that go along with it.

And what does a new area offer outside of work? Recreational activities, entertainment, and cultural opportunities should be taken into consideration. Talk with your potential co-workers to find out what you might or might not like about the social climate. Explore your potential new area as much as possible. Take a day to drive around and visit some places and individuals you might want to become familiar with—local churches, parks, schools and teachers, volunteer organizations, retail establishments, and neighborhood restaurants.

What's the weather like in your new town? Are you used to sun? Do you like to ski? Do you like the rain? Do you want a white Christmas? Know the climate and know what you like.

Finally if you decide to make the move, who will pay for it? In some cases your new company will—but understand that this is not automatic. Make sure you inquire about a potential employer's relocation policies before accepting a position. A cross-country move can cost up to $5,000.

Factors to consider before you make the move:

- Salary
- Comparative cost of living
- Relocation expenses
- Transportation
- Weather
- Environmental quality
- Spouse/family concerns
- Access to house of worship
- Political climate
- Availability/quality of schools

Just as a new job is a learning experience, so is living in a different part of the country. Your first full-time job is a perfect time to experience new surroundings, especially with the understanding that in today's job market, nothing is forever.

▲ Conclusion

You should now feel much more comfortable in answering the question, "What are you worth?" Being the recipient of multiple job offers is a great honor. Take your time in evaluating these offers and choose the one that meets the greatest number of your needs and values.

▲ Activity

Now that you have learned about negotiating salaries, it is time for you to conduct some research. Visit your campus career center. More than likely, the career center will have salary data for your region, your school's alumni, and/or for the nation. Research salary ranges for your major and your career field of interest. Also, research the cost of living in the region of the country or world where you would like to relocate. Adjust the salary range for your field according to the cost of living for your desired location. Think of the skills that you have that other candidates may not possess. How will these impact your desired starting salary? Consider other reasons that you should adjust your starting salary until you arrive at a range that you feel is appropriate. Armed with this information, you can better evaluate job offers and you will be prepared to answer the salary question if it is asked during an interview.

References

Bohac, Jennifer (1998). Dissertation: *Occupational Progress and Career Planning of Former Student-Athletes in the Newly Created Big 12 Conference.*

Breidenbach, Monica E. (1992). *Career Development: Taking Charge of Your Career.* Englewood Cliffs, NJ: Prentice Hall.

Bruce, Calvin E. (March–April 1993). "Discovering the Hidden Job Market." *The Black Collegian*, pp. 84–86.

Ellis, Dave et al. *Career Planning.* (1990). Rapid City, SD: College Survival.

Kennedy, Joyce Lain, and Thomas J. Morrow (1994). *Electronic Resume Revolution.* John Wiley & Son, Inc., New York.

Kouzes, James, and Barry Posner (1987). *The Leadership Challenge.* San Francisco: Jossey-Bass.

The National Employment Weekly. (August 3, 1996). "Advice on Writing Resumes That Can Be Scanned Easily."

NCAA (1995). *NCAA Life Skills Program Notebook: Life After Sports.* Overland Park, KS: NCAA.

Positioning Yourself for Success: An Employment Counseling Handbook for Athletes (1990). U.S. Olympic Committee.

Sanders, Eric J. (Fall 1992). "Implementing a Career Development Program for Student-Athletes." *Academic Athletic Journal.* pp. 25–29.

Satterfield, M. (1993). *How to Negotiate the Raise You Deserve.* Horizons, Lincolnwood, IL: VGM Career Horizons.

Schindler, Pamela. (Winter 1997). "Demonstrating Competence: The Portfolio Interview for Management Positions." *JOURNAL.* pp. 44–46.

SIGI PLUS. (1992). *User's Guide.* Princeton Educational Testing Service.

Sweet, Meriby. (Nov.–Dec. 1992). "Making the Most of Your Summer Opportunities." *The Black Collegian.* pp. 100–105

Texas State Occupational Information Coordinating Committee. (1983) *Texas Job Hunter's Guide.* Austin, TX: Texas SOICC.

Tieger, P.D., and B. Barron-Tieger (1992). *Do What You Are.* New York, Little, Brown and Company.

Index

A

Academics, importance of, 10–11
Activities
    attire, selecting, 117
    cover letter writing, 111
    internet search, 170
    interviewing, 159
    job offer, 189
    networking, 89, 91–92
    résumé writing, 80–81
    self-assessment, 34
    transitioning, 2–5, 12–13
    values assessment, 19–22, 23–25
Applications, job, 109–111
Assessment
    career
        instruments used, 25–28
        shadowing, 29–34
    self, 15–16
        four-year career plan and, 38–39
        informal, 16
        skills, 16–19
        values, 19–25

C

Campbell Interest and Skill Survey, 26
Career planning
    advice for, 42–43
    four-year, 36, 38–41
Co-op, 174, 175
Cover letter, 102–108, 111

D

Dictionary of Occupational Titles, 98
Discover, 26

E

Employers
    expectations of, 54
    qualities they look for, 6–7, 51–52
    researching, 93–97
Experience, professional
    co-op, 174, 175
    internships, 173–174, 175
    programs, 172

I

Internet, use of, 161–169
Internships, 173–174, 175
Interview
  business etiquette during, 114–117
  checklist, final, 142–144
  dressing for, 112–114
  first impressions, 122–124
  follow-up, 155–157
  informational, 29–34
  phases of, 119
  preparing for, 52–53, 120–122
  questions
    to ask the interviewer, 137–138
    negative, responding to, 134–137
    standard, 124–134
  research information as an aid, 99–101
  storytelling, art of, 139–141
  tips from on-campus recruiters, 144–145
  types of, 145–147
    behavioral interviews, 146, 147–152

J

Job market research, conducting, 97–99
Job offers
  multiple, 180–182
  negotiating salary and, 176–180
  responding to, 182–183
    sample letters, 184–186
Job search
  advice from former student-athletes, 8–11
  applications, completing, 109–111
  assessing your skills, 11, 12–13
  conduction of, 46–51
  employers
    expectations of, 54
    qualities they look for, 6–7, 51–52
    researching, 97
  four-year career plan, 36, 38–41
  internet, use of, 161–169
  interview
    business etiquette during, 114–117
    checklist, final, 142–144
    dressing for, 112–114
    first impressions, 122–124
    follow-up, 155–157
    informational, 29–34
    phases of, 119
    preparing for, 52–53, 120–122
    questions
      to ask the interviewer, 137–138
      negative, responding to, 134–137
      standard, 124–134
    research information as an aid, 99–101
    storytelling, art of, 139–141
    tips from on-campus recruiters, 144–145
    types of, 145–147
      behavioral interviews, 146, 147–152
  job market research, 97–99
  letters of recommendation, 89–91
  marketing plan, 45–46
  networking
    appropriate, 83
    conducting a job search and, 47
    contacts
      making new, 83–84
      meeting with, 84–85
    maintenance tips, 85–86
    parties and, 88–89
    school, 9
    skills, 86–88
  nine-step approach, 42–43
  portfolio, 78–80
  qualities an employer looks for, 6–7, 51–52

Index

rejection, dealing with, 158–159
résumé
  action words used in, 74–77
  college student's, 62–64
  cover letters and, 102–108, 111
  online résumé bank, 167
  pointers, 77–78
  preparation of, 64–66, 71
    format, 61–62
  samples, 67–70, 74
  scannable, 71–74
  worksheet, 36, 37
site visit, 152–155
strategies, 43–45
technology, use of, 160–170
telephone use and, 55–59

M

Myers-Briggs Type Indicator, 26

N

NCAA, transition techniques, 2–5
Networking
  appropriate, 83
  conducting a job search and, 47
  contacts
    making new, 83–84
    meeting with, 84–85
  maintenance tips, 85–86
  parties and, 88–89
  school, 9
  skills, 86–88

O

Occupational Outlook Handbook, 98–99

P

Portfolio, 78–80
Professional athletes, the work of, 5–6
Professional experience
  co-op, 174, 175
  internships, 173–174, 175
  programs, 172

R

Recommendation, letters of, 89–91
Rejection, dealing with, 158–159
Relocation, 187–188
Résumé (*see* job search)

S

Salary, negotiation of, 176–180
SIGI-Plus, 25, 27–28
Site visit, 152–155
Skills
  assessment of, 16–19
  networking, 86–88
  transferable, 6–7, 11, 13
Sports
  transitioning activities, 2–5
  websites, 167–169
Strong Interest Inventory, 26–27

T

Technology, use of, 160–170
Telephone use and the job search, 55–59
Thank-you letter format, 156–157

V

Values, assessment of, 19–25

W

Web sites
   career, 162–167
   sports related, 167–169
Worksheet
   behavioral interview, 149–152
   informational interviewing, 32–33
   multiple job offers, 182–183
   résumé, 36, 37
   skills, transferable, 11, 13